Epic
of
Gilgamesh

Anonymous

ISBN: 9798883987242

CONTENTS

1 THE REIGN OF GILGAMESH AND THE

DAWN OF A RIVAL

Under the protective shade of a hedge, as the fires of high noon began to wane, the barley earth, ripened by the sun of the plain, became the silent witness of an ancient story about to be told. In this field, where the golden grains swayed gently to the rhythm of the wind, the story of Gilgamesh, a king of unparalleled greatness, was to be unveiled. Gilgamesh was not an easy name to pronounce, with its Sumerian sound demanding that one practice rolling it in the mouth, swallowing it, until it filled the chest, mingling with every breath, with every bit of life.

Gilgamesh ruled over Uruk, a powerful city of Mesopotamia, feared by its neighbors and protected by an imposing wall of bricks topped with nine hundred towers. This capital, fertile and vibrant, stretched over a thousand hectares of gardens, orchards, and enclosures for livestock, bordered by fish-filled ponds, majestic temples, sumptuous palaces, and bustling neighborhoods. The Euphrates, after its long journey from the snows of Armenia, flowed peacefully through it, its waters cradled by the boats of boatmen, making this land a true Garden of Eden.

In this kingdom, Gilgamesh imposed his will, accountable for his actions only to the gods themselves, the true sovereigns of this land. Under the protection of Anu, the greatest of the gods, and Ishtar, the goddess of love and war, the king seemed untouchable. Yet, despite this divine protection, Uruk knew no peace, for Gilgamesh, in his brutality and authoritarianism, gave his people no respite. His hand was heavy, and his desires, insatiable. He constantly levied on the city's riches, creating taxes, imposing corvées, and sowing terror when he walked the streets with his band of rogue courtiers.

The inhabitants of Uruk, desperate, implored the gods to free them from their tyrant. The gods, having shaped the world and humanity from a clump of clay and their own blood, could not remain indifferent to these prayers. Despite the favor enjoyed by Gilgamesh, they had to find a way to contain his arrogance without destroying him.

The cries of despair from the people of Uruk rose to the gates of heaven, mixing with the mocking laughter of Gilgamesh, who boasted of his likeness to the gods. But the divinities, concerned for the fate of men, decided to act. During a celestial assembly, Anu, the father of the gods, proposed the idea of a rival for Gilgamesh. Ea, the divine engineer, seized this idea and turned to Aruru the Great, the mother of all creation, to shape this rival from her ancient mold of life.

Thus, in the steppe, far from the sight of men and gods, a plan was implemented to create a being capable of rivaling Gilgamesh, to teach him humility, and to restore balance in the city of Uruk. It was the beginning of a new era for Uruk, an era where the fate of Gilgamesh would take an unexpected turn, thanks to divine intervention and the birth of an unparalleled rival.

The creation of this rival marked the beginning of a new era for Uruk, an era where Gilgamesh's unshakeable arrogance would be put to the test. The gods, in their infinite wisdom, had decided it was time for the king to meet his equal, a being who could not only rival him in strength and courage but could also teach him the value of humility and compassion. In the sacred depths of the earth, Aruru, the Great Mother, mixed her divine essence with the clay of creation. With a delicacy and precision that belonged only to the gods, she shaped Gilgamesh's rival. This new being, named Enkidu, was both wild and noble, endowed with supernatural strength and a raw beauty. He was the incarnation of pristine and untamed nature, a striking contrast to the civilization over which Gilgamesh reigned.

Enkidu, initially ignorant of the ways of men, lived among the wild beasts, sharing their water, their food, and their company. His presence in the steppe did not go unnoticed, and soon, rumors of this wild man reached Uruk. Gilgamesh, intrigued and perhaps for the first time in his life, felt the echo of a challenge he could not ignore.

The meeting between Gilgamesh and Enkidu was not one of enemies but rather of souls destined to be bound in a way that neither could have anticipated. Their initial confrontation, full of strength and fury, quickly turned into a mutual recognition of their kindred spirits. Enkidu, with his purity and connection to nature, brought Gilgamesh a perspective he had never considered, pushing him to question not only the way he ruled over his people but also the nature of his own being.

From this meeting, a deep friendship was born, a brotherhood forged through trials and adventures they shared. Together, they explored the limits of their world, facing monsters and challenges that would have defeated mere mortals. Each victory brought them closer, teaching them the value of trust, sacrifice, and brotherly love.

However, the destiny of Gilgamesh and Enkidu was woven with joy and sorrow, light and shadow. The challenges they faced together prepared them for a trial that would test not only their strength but also the depth of their bond. The quest for immortality, the confrontation with their own mortality, and ultimately, the heartbreaking loss and the search for eternal wisdom, marked the last chapter of their journey together.

In the pages of this ancient epic, the story of Gilgamesh and Enkidu unfolds as a mirror of humanity's aspirations, fears, and hopes. Through their tale, the ancient narratives remind us of the timeless lessons on the nature of friendship, the weight of power, and man's ceaseless quest to find his place in the vastness of a universe that, while full of wonders, remains indifferent to the dreams and desires of mortals.

2 DAWN OF A COMPANION

Across the vast plain, the barley swayed with the wind, while further afield, fields of rapeseed edged the horizon, their pods nearly ripe, capturing the light. The breeze, in its irregular movements, seemed to seek refuge, as if a spirit animated the wind. This idea, though strange, invited one to perceive the plain through the eyes of the Ancients, for whom every breath of air and every vibration of the earth was inhabited.

Beyond this fertile plain lay an arid steppe. A landscape of bare pastures, sparse bushes, and trees frozen in silence, where the dust stirred by a passing herd, the distant roar of a lion, or the hasty flight of gazelles would disrupt the tranquility. In the distance, shepherd fires punctuated the barren expanse, and the golden light of the sun danced on the course of a river.

It was in this inhospitable steppe that Ea and Aruru chose to settle to accomplish their promised work: the creation of a rudimentary being, a man of a single block, with compact and hard fiber, within whom would burn a quiet flame, heralding the dawn. Ea, without hesitation, set to work, digging the earth before mixing his saliva with the clay, an ancestral gesture that once required the sacrifice of a god to breathe life into the first humanity. This time, the mere essence of Ea was enough to trigger the creation process.

As Ea kneaded the earth, Aruru sang a song that enveloped the steppe, soothing all life around, concentrating the divine essence in the act of creation. They were alone, the gods, in their open-air workshop, giving shape to a new life.

Gradually, the creature took form under Aruru's hands, who, after shaping the body, used a tamarisk twig to breathe the spark of life into the inert dough. Together, Ea and Aruru observed the result of their labor, wondering what future awaited this creation destined to become Gilgamesh's rival.

In the silence of the steppe, life awakened in the body of the newly formed being. The earth enveloping it began to crack, revealing rough skin beneath the bark. The chest rose with the rhythm of a nascent breath, and soon, Enkidu, for that was his name now, issued his first cry, discovering the power of his voice.

Astonished and moved by this discovery, Enkidu began to walk, his clumsy steps resonating like a primitive dance on the steppe's earth. His life began under the benevolent gaze of the gods who, satisfied, withdrew, leaving behind them an indelible mark on the fate of the earth.

Meanwhile, in his palace, Gilgamesh was troubled by prophetic dreams. Startled awake by disturbing visions, he called to his mother, the goddess Ninsun, to illuminate the meaning of his dreams. She appeared to him, assuring him that these dreams heralded the arrival of a powerful friend, a companion with whom he would form an invincible duo. Reassured, Gilgamesh fell back asleep, still unaware of Enkidu's existence and the upheaval his arrival would cause.

Soon after, a hunter came to disturb the king's peace with news of a strange creature ravaging his hunting lands.The description of this being, wild and powerful, living among the beasts, resembling a man but endowed with the strength of a mountain, struck Gilgamesh. The hunter, with words imbued with respectful fear, painted the image of Enkidou, a being of noble savagery, protector of gazelles, hunter of lions with bare hands, a being with skin hardened by the elements and hair tangled with earth. A being who, despite his brute appearance, reflected a power that matched that of Gilgamesh, the Bull of Uruk.

Gilgamesh listened, captivated and troubled by the hunter's tale. The dreams that had agitated him suddenly took shape; the stone fallen from the sky, the axe he could not lift, all symbols of this stranger who came to disturb the balance of his world. A vivid, almost divine force seemed to emanate from the description of this wild creature, and a burning curiosity took hold of him. He felt a mix of envy and challenge, a thirst to confront this force, to face it, to tame it, perhaps even to unite with it to forge an unshakable alliance.

Gilgamesh's initial anger turned into firm resolution. He was already devising a plan to capture this force of nature, to bend it to his will, or perhaps, to learn from it. The idea of a rival, of a companion of this stature, transformed his restlessness into a feverish anticipation. For the first time in his life, Gilgamesh, the undisputed king, the invincible warrior, contemplated the possibility of equality, even brotherhood with another.

The days that followed were marked by an electricity-laden wait. Gilgamesh, accustomed to command, to dominate, now found himself in a position of expectancy, scanning the horizon for the appearance of this Enkidou, this being who had already transformed his reality without even having set foot within the walls of his city.

And as Gilgamesh navigated between impatience and introspection, the wheels of fate continued to turn. The dreams that had visited him were not mere nocturnal echoes; they were omens of a meeting that would not only define the course of his life but also that of the history of Uruk. Enkidou, with his miraculous birth orchestrated by the gods, was not merely destined to be a rival for Gilgamesh; he was to become his greatest ally, his brother-in-arms, in an epic that would resonate through the ages.

In this wait, Uruk stood on the threshold of a new era, an era where two forces of nature, two demigods, would unite their destinies to forge an immortal legend. The arrival of Enkidou, as brutal and unexpected as it might seem, was the prelude to a profound transformation, not only for Gilgamesh but for the entire kingdom of Uruk.

3 THE TRANSFORMATION OF ENKIDU

Gilgamesh, the king of Uruk, had devised a cunning plan to tame the wild spirit of Enkidu, his equal in strength but not yet in humanity. The idea had come to him in the solitude of his palace, as he meditated on the untamed nature of Enkidu, a being shaped by the harshness of the steppe, nourished by its flora and fauna, speaking the language of the wind and wild beasts. Gilgamesh knew that to domesticate him, he needed to lure him into a new life, to disconnect him from this primitive source that was his own.

Thus, Gilgamesh went to the temple of Ishtar, where he implored the aid of the priestess, the servant of the goddess of love and war. He entrusted her with his mission: to find Enkidu in the vastness of the steppe and awaken him to his true nature, that of a man. The priestess, understanding the magnitude of the task, prepared carefully, perfuming her skin and donning a linen tunic, before setting off towards the steppe, driven by royal determination.

In the open expanse, Enkidu lived free, running with the gazelles and leading them. The priestess first observed him from a distance, admiring the brutal simplicity of his existence, until she approached close enough to capture his attention. At the sight of this ethereal figure, Enkidu, intrigued but wary, stopped, allowing the priestess to come closer.

When she was close enough, she revealed herself to him in all her vulnerability, causing in Enkidu an awakening of senses he had never experienced before. Touching her skin, smelling her scent, everything about her irresistibly drew him towards a reality he had not yet explored. Under the guidance of Ishtar's priestess, Enkidu discovered love, that powerful force that transforms and unites, under the benevolent gaze of the gods themselves.

Their union was celebrated by the heavens, Shamash and Ishtar sending their blessings in the form of winged creatures and twinkling stars, marking Enkidu's transformation. From a solitary wild being, he became a being capable of love, jealousy, fear of solitude - a man in all his complexity.

This intense and revealing love was the catalyst that changed Enkidou. Under the tamarisk tree, alongside the priestess, he opened up to a new existence, marking the beginning of a journey that would take him far from the steppe, towards unimaginable destinies. In this intimate communion, Enkidou found not only love but also a new path, paved with human emotions, that would guide him towards his inevitable meeting with Gilgamesh, and beyond, towards adventures that would inscribe them both into legend.

The steppe was swept by a powerful wind, a harbinger of change, driving away the gazelles and all the fauna that had until then been close to Enkidou and the priestess in their budding intimacy. The air was charged with a new tension, as if nature itself sensed Enkidou's imminent awakening to his new life.

On the seventh day, as dawn painted fresh colors across the horizon, Enkidou woke from a deep sleep, the priestess resting peacefully by his side. He watched her, marveling at the gentleness of her presence, almost timidly touching the surface of this new reality that unfolded before him. The silent exchange of glances was enough to confirm that a threshold had been crossed; Enkidou was transformed.

Rising, he gazed at the steppe stretching out before him, vast and familiar, yet now tinged with subtle nostalgia. He attempted to rejoin his former companions, the gazelles, eager to share his renewed joy. Yet, the distance between them had irrevocably widened. As he tried to approach them, their graceful silhouettes receded, leaving him alone against the wild expanse. His muscles, once tireless, betrayed a new weariness; something within him had irrevocably changed.

Overwhelmed, Enkidou knelt down, allowing tears to flow freely for the first time, marking his passage from savagery to humanity. The priestess, approaching, offered him a look filled with understanding and compassion. "You are born anew," she whispered to him, her words falling like seeds into the fertile soil of his being.

Enkidou struggled to grasp the scope of these words, his mind still entangled in the threads of his past life. "Man," he articulated, exploring the weight of this new identity with childlike curiosity. "Woman," he repeated, touching the priestess, then himself, as if to anchor this reality through touch.

In a burst of raw joy, he lifted her, spinning her in the air before embracing her against him, a wild laugh escaping his throat. "Enkidou, man. Woman, gazelle. Together," he proclaimed, each word adding a layer to his newly forged identity.

As they prepared to leave the steppe, the priestess warned him that his path would now lead him to Uruk, to a life among men, to Gilgamesh. "You are born and he awaits you," she said, planting in him the promise of a meeting that would forever change the course of their destiny.

The journey to Uruk took them through encampments where Enkidou was welcomed as a living omen, his reputation having preceded him through the whispers of the steppe. The priestess seized this opportunity to introduce him to human customs, teaching him to eat bread, a symbol of his belonging to the community of men. Enkidou, faced with this foreign food, initially showed reluctance, but under the encouragement of the priestess, he endeavored to adopt this new facet of his identity.

Thus, step by step, Enkidou drew closer to Uruk, carrying with him the lessons of the steppe and the hopes of a life renewed among men, guided by the promise of a friendship that would resonate through the ages.

Enkidou, with childlike hesitation, again accepts the bread from the woman, chewing laboriously under her benevolent gaze. When she offers him a jug of beer, presenting this bitter drink as a rite of passage into humanity, Enkidou is struck with nausea. The beer, a symbol of civilization, contrasts with the purity of the steppe waters he is accustomed to. Encouraged by the woman, he tries again, letting the drink and its effects transform him, the alcohol clouding his senses, bringing him closer to the man he is meant to become.

Their journey leads them to the gates of Uruk, the city of men, where a dense and noisy crowd welcomes them. The woman, agile and determined, leads the way through the narrow alleys, while Enkidou, clumsy in his new garb, follows as best he can, overwhelmed by the weight of his transformation. His voice rises in the urban cacophony, calling to the one who guided him here, but she does not turn back, leaving Enkidou to face his new world alone.

Enkidou's fame precedes him, the voice of the steppe having announced his arrival. The townspeople, in awe, crowd around him, touching the one who was once a legend. Enkidou, lost without his guide, is swept away by the human tide, his heart heavy with loss and uncertainty.

In a heart-wrenching cry, he calls out one last time to the woman, his voice breaking under the weight of emotion. But the crowd, indifferent to his distress, sees in him only the promise of a meeting with Gilgamesh, their indomitable king. Enkidou, alone amidst the tumult of Uruk, stands at the crossroads, his old life behind him and a new destiny, still shrouded in uncertainty, unfolding before him.

4 THE MAKING OF BROTHERS

In the dusty alleys of Uruk, a palpable tension floated in the air as Gilgamesh, the untamed king, made his way through the city, closely followed by his band of loyalists. Their destination was none other than a wedding celebration, an occasion Gilgamesh was accustomed to appropriating with audacity bordering on insolence. According to a controversial tradition, he claimed the right to share the bride's bed before even her husband, under the spurious pretext of blessing the lands of Uruk with his royal virility. This custom, far from being a mark of favor, sowed desolation and dismay among the citizens, a reality Gilgamesh greeted with cruel indifference.

Their march was punctuated by acts of wanton vandalism, overturning everything in their path, from simple herds to the humble trade of artisans. These acts of depredation heralded the imminent arrival of Gilgamesh, spreading a shockwave of fear and indignation across the city. It was in this climate of anticipated terror that news of their approach reached Enkidou, elevated in triumph by a group of desperate inhabitants, thirsty for justice.

The confrontation seemed inevitable. As Gilgamesh advanced, confident in his divine right, he was brought to an abrupt halt by the resounding cry of Enkidou, a figure as imposing as himself, emanating raw strength and unwavering determination. In the flash of a moment, silence fell, the very air holding its breath, as the two titans faced each other.

Enkidou, his face marked by the stigmas of the steppe, embodied a pure and untamed force of nature. Before him stood Gilgamesh, the all-powerful king, in all his royal splendor, yet troubled by the presence of this unexpected equal. Enkidou, with an authority that brooked no contest, reminded Gilgamesh to respect the most sacred of traditions, those of marriage and conjugal union.

The tension between the two men was palpable, their bodies ready for confrontation. But it was not a race or a headlong charge that launched them against each other. No, it was a walk, heavy and determined, the very ground seeming to tremble under the weight of their confrontation.

When Enkidou grabbed Gilgamesh, it was with a strength that matched his own, their hands coming down with a power that echoed the fury of their hearts. For the first time, Gilgamesh met someone whose will and strength could rival his own, a worthy opponent. In this embrace, there was not only the promise of a battle but the beginning of an epic that would define their destiny and that of the entirety of Uruk.

The fight between Gilgamesh and Enkidou, like a furious storm, shook the foundations of Uruk. Their bodies, locked together in a merciless struggle, were the stage for a battle as ancient as time itself. They roared in fury, each promising the ruin of the other, their voices merging with the crash of their confrontation.

The crowd, captivated and horrified, formed a circle around them, pulsating to the rhythm of their combat. Encouragements for Enkidou flew, fueled by the burning desire to see Gilgamesh defeated. War cries and cries of victory rose, while the two combatants, absorbed in their duel, seemed deaf to the excitement surrounding them.

As their struggle led them through the districts of Uruk, leaving behind a trail of destruction, they finally reached the main square, under the impassive gaze of the temples of Anu and Ishtar. There, the battle reached its climax. Gilgamesh, a master in the art of combat, deployed all his cunning and agility, while Enkidu, a brute force of nature, responded with relentless resistance, backing down at nothing.

Despite Gilgamesh's mastery, Enkidou held firm, his unwavering determination keeping him from defeat. The crowd, witnessing this spectacle, oscillated between hope and despair, uttering cries of joy and disappointment, according to the turns of the duel.

But, in a moment of epiphany, as Gilgamesh seemed on the verge of being overpowered, the crowd held its breath. Enkidou, faced with the possibility of overthrowing the king, hesitated. His gaze lost in that of Gilgamesh, he discovered an unsuspected nobility, a shared humanity that made him doubt his own rage.

Calls for Enkidou to take Gilgamesh's place echoed around them, but in Enkidou's heart, a different melody was heard - that of the wind, the rain, the wild world from which he came. How could he, a child of the steppes, rule over the complexity of a city like Uruk?

Suddenly, the tension broke. Gilgamesh, taking advantage of Enkidou's hesitation, freed himself and, in a gesture of rediscovered brotherhood, raised his opponent's arm as if to proclaim him the victor. "I have found my equal!" he exclaimed, transforming their confrontation into a celebration of their equality.

The crowd, stunned, fell silent, faced with an unexpected outcome. Whispers of disappointment and questioning mingled with reflections on what this new alliance between the Bull of Uruk and the Lion of the steppe would mean. And as criticism and praise faded into the twilight of Uruk, Gilgamesh and Enkidou, united by a battle that had transcended violence to become a bond of mutual respect, stood side by side, ready to face together the challenges to come.

In the paved streets of Uruk, under the imposing shadow of temples and ziggurats piercing the sky, a palpable tension permeated the air. The citizens, faces marked by trials, gathered in the great square, watched with an intensity mixed with hope and despair the outcome of a confrontation that had captured the essence of their daily struggle against the tyranny of Gilgamesh.

Imagine yourself there, among them, whether you are a fisherman pulling your nets from the tumultuous waters of the Euphrates, a basket weaver deftly interlacing the reeds of the marshes, or a scribe, carefully engraving exploits and decrees on clay tablets. Each, in their heart, carried the weight of a life shaped by the will of a king whose whims and cruelty seemed boundless.

The inhabitants of Uruk had long implored the gods for relief, a sign, a divine intervention that could end their suffering. And when Enkidou appeared, like a living omen sent by those same deities, a ripple of hope ran through the crowd. In him, they saw the promise of change, the emergence of a force capable of challenging Gilgamesh, of restoring balance and justice to their exhausted world.

Yet, before their eyes, this hope seemed to waver. Enkidou, the champion of the oppressed, hesitated, his immense strength held back by an inner revelation that turned him away from the path of vengeance and domination. In his choice to renounce violence, to ascend to power without bloodshed, the citizens perceived not weakness, but a profound enigma, a dilemma that touched them all at heart.

The gods of Sumer, these omnipresent entities in every aspect of life, from the germination of seeds in the fields to protection against storms and floods, seemed to have offered and then withdrawn their blessing in the same breath. The prayers, sacrifices, rituals observed with unwavering devotion had brought only a moment of relief, an illusion of salvation before plunging the citizens back into an abyss of uncertainty.

Enkidou's reaction to Gilgamesh, turning their confrontation into a mutual recognition of strength and worth, left the spectators in a state of perplexity. What did this turnaround mean? Was it the end of their quest for justice, or the beginning of a new era, forged not by conquest, but by understanding and agreement?

As cries and whispers faded, each returned home, carrying within them these questions, this reflection on the meaning of struggle, resilience, and forgiveness. Night fell on Uruk, enveloping its inhabitants in a precarious tranquility, a moment of peace to meditate on the lessons of a day that would remain engraved in the collective memory of the eternal city.

5 FORGING DESTINY

In the beating heart of Uruk, under the majestic vaults of the royal palace, an unlikely friendship was woven between Gilgamesh, the all-powerful ruler, and Enkidou, once the wild embodiment of the vast steppic expanses. The union of these two beings, forged in adversity and sealed by mutual respect, promised to redefine the destiny not only of their own lives but also of the entire kingdom.

Had the gods, in their enigmatic wisdom, anticipated the course of these events? Had they foreseen the profound effect this alliance would have on Uruk and its inhabitants? It seemed that even the deities had left a part to chance, thus allowing freedom and choice to shape the thread of destinies.

Gilgamesh, in a gesture of affection and protection, welcomed Enkidou into the splendors of his palace. He offered him an apartment adjacent to his own, surrounded by devoted servants, and ensured his friend was bathed, perfumed, and clothed in garments worthy of the royal court. These attentions, far removed from the image of the destroyer Gilgamesh had once embodied, revealed a hitherto unknown facet of his personality.

Why did Gilgamesh, so prone to violence and domination, choose to shield Enkidou from any corruption, as if in him, he had recognized a pure reflection of his own being? This question remained pending, evoking the complexity of the bonds that now united the two men.

Enkidou, for his part, found himself immersed in a world radically different from anything he had known. His days spent alongside Gilgamesh were filled with discoveries and learning: the management of the kingdom, military strategy, diplomacy. Gilgamesh introduced him at court as to a son, perhaps preparing him to one day share the responsibilities of the throne.

However, despite the warmth of their friendship and Gilgamesh's generosity, Enkidou felt a growing void. The luxurious baths, intoxicating perfumes, and rich fabrics could not replace the freedom and authenticity of life on the steppe. His mind, once sharp and alert, became muddled in the complexities and intrigues of the court, his body, once capable of challenging wild beasts, grew heavy with delicate dishes and inactivity.

The streets of Uruk buzzed with rumors about their king's transformation. Some saw in the friendship between Gilgamesh and Enkidou a harbinger of peace and prosperity, while others feared that Gilgamesh's old demons might resurface, more destructive than ever. Whatever the truth, the fragile balance between the two friends seemed destined to be tested, their souls intertwined in a complex dance where each step could either draw them closer or push them forever apart from the harmony for which they had fought so hard.

In the golden splendor of Uruk's palace, Gilgamesh desperately sought to rekindle the spirit of Enkidou, his friend and fellow warrior, whose melancholy thickened with each passing day. Watching Enkidou wander through the city streets, accepting offerings and flatteries from the citizens but never regaining the spark of joy that once lit up his gaze, Gilgamesh felt a weight on his heart.

To please Enkidou, Gilgamesh introduced him to other women, perhaps hoping to awaken in him the memory of the passion he had known with the woman of the watering hole. But none could compete with the memory of that sunlit encounter, those moments stolen from eternity where Enkidou had tasted true love.

Gilgamesh, observing Enkidou lose his appetite for the life they led within the palace walls, understood that the pleasures of city life would not suffice to heal his friend's soul. He knew that Enkidou longed for the limitless freedom of the steppe, for the caress of the wind in his hair and the burning sun on his skin, for the intimate communion with the earth that spoke to his feet.

With a sudden inspiration, Gilgamesh conceived a bold plan, a challenge worthy of their burgeoning legend. He proposed to Enkidou a distant expedition, a journey that would take them far beyond the known borders of their world, to the Cedar Mountain, to face Humbaba, the monstrous guardian of the forest. Enkidou, initially invigorated by the idea of the adventure, faltered under the weight of his terrifying memories of Humbaba, a being of formidable magical power, against whom he had once measured himself, without success.

Gilgamesh, however, was not discouraged by Enkidou's fears. With gentleness and persuasion, he reminded Enkidou that he was no longer the same man as before, that together, united by an unbreakable bond and blessed by the gods themselves, they could overcome any obstacle. He invoked the divine aura conferred by his lineage, the protection of their goddess mother, to convince Enkidou that their victory was not only possible but predestined.

Enkidou, listening to Gilgamesh's passionate words, gradually became swept up in his friend's vision. Gilgamesh's stories painted a picture where glory and heroism awaited them, where their names would be sung through the ages as those of the greatest heroes. And in Gilgamesh's eyes, Enkidou saw not only the flame of determination but also the reflection of their deep friendship, a bond that transcended fear and doubt.

Finally, Enkidou's heart lightened, and with a renewed smile, he agreed to embark on this perilous quest alongside Gilgamesh. Together, they would prepare to write a new chapter in their legend, a tale of friendship, courage, and combat against the forces that stood in their way to immortality.

6 THE QUEST BEGINS: TRIUMPH AND TRIAL

The announcement of Gilgamesh and Enkidou's bold venture spread like wildfire through the paved streets of Uruk, stirring a mix of admiration and disbelief among its inhabitants. For the first time, Gilgamesh's actions were met not with tears but with cheers. The entire city seemed to vibrate with palpable excitement at the idea of their quest to defeat Humbaba, the dreaded guardian of the Cedar Forest.

A celebration was quickly organized, gathering the community beyond the rampart, in the sacred enclosure where the earth was traditionally awakened from its winter slumber. The festivity had an air of defiance, as if by honoring the departure of the heroes, one hoped to harvest not only glory but also a crop of legends for the posterity of Uruk.

The city's sages joined the celebration, offering their advice tinged with concern to Gilgamesh. They warned him of the cunning and power of Humbaba, whose domain stretched over hundreds of miles, a territory closely watched by this monster on the orders of the gods. They emphasized caution, the importance of fresh water, and the attentive listening to dreams, those cryptic messages sent by the divinities.

But Enkidou's mind was already far away, traversing the perilous paths of their future odyssey. Gilgamesh, for his part, escaped the heaviness of the warnings to turn towards more spiritual thoughts, invoking the protection of Shamash for their journey. In the sanctuary, he felt the reassuring presence of his mother, Ninsun, imploring the sun god to watch over her son.

Gilgamesh's prayers were imbued with a newfound humility. He asked Shamash not only to guide him but also to help him understand the divine signs, aware of the significance of their undertaking. He aspired to achieve something great, something that would transcend his brute strength and his skill in deception, something that would be remembered long after his disappearance.

When they left the temple, an arsenal worthy of this quest awaited them. Magnificent weapons, specially forged for the occasion, glittered in the sunlight. Their brilliance rivaled the splendor of the firmament. Each piece of equipment, from the axe to the large cutlass, was a work of art, promising strength and protection to its bearers.

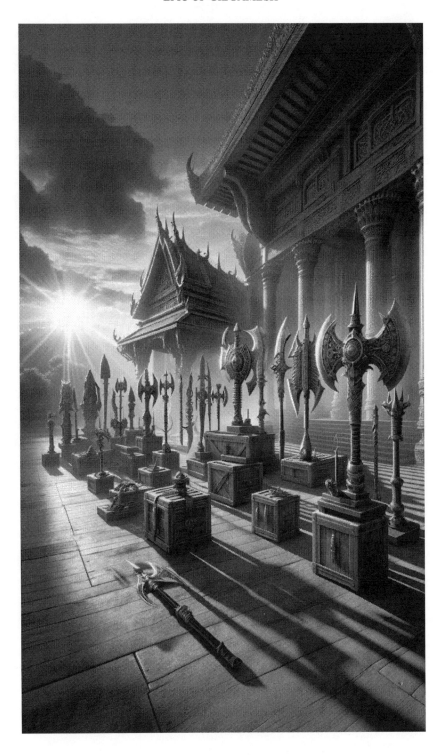

With solemn gravity, Gilgamesh and Enkidou donned their armor. Under the weight of expectations and their gear, they gave one last salute to the crowd before heading towards their fate. Their departure was like a flash; in a few powerful strides, they crossed the boundaries of Uruk, leaving behind a city suspended between hope and anxiety.

The steppe welcomed them, vast and untamed. Each step took them further away from civilization, drawing them closer to the wild heart of the world and their inevitable confrontation with Humbaba. The heroes, carried by fierce determination and the blessing of the gods, soon disappeared from view, swallowed by the immensity of nature calling them.

***

Gilgamesh and Enkidou advanced with fierce determination, covering distances with superhuman ease. Enkidou, leading their way, set a brisk pace that Gilgamesh followed without faltering. The steppe, vast and wild, seemed to welcome them like lost sons returning home. It whispered greetings to Enkidou, the son of nature it had watched grow. The grasses gently bowed under their steps, gazelles raised their heads at their passing, and even the lions offered roars of welcome. The entire earth recognized Enkidou, and through him, it welcomed Gilgamesh.

Enkidou, revitalized by his return to his element, transformed before Gilgamesh's eyes. He moved with a grace that belied his imposing stature, each step in harmony with the breath of the steppe. He no longer walked; he danced with the wind, recharging with every breath of the pure air of nature.

Gilgamesh, though less at ease in this wild environment, endeavored to keep up with Enkidou's pace, learning from him to listen and synchronize with the ancient rhythms of the earth. Together, they covered prodigious distances, stopping only to replenish before resuming their race against time.

The sun, their constant companion, finally set, dipping into the distant sea, while Shamash entrusted the care of his proteges to the stars. In the evening, Enkidou tended to the fire, while Gilgamesh prepared their simple yet nourishing meal. Fresh water from a well they dug with their own hands quenched their thirst and purified their feet, connecting them even more deeply to the land that had seen them born.

Enkidou's hunting, instinctive and agile, provided a vital supplement to their diet. When he captured prey with the speed of a natural predator, his joyful laughter echoed in the twilight. He offered Gilgamesh to share this raw meal, a symbol of the raw strength of the steppe, but Gilgamesh, although tempted, could not bring himself to embrace this wild custom.

This shared moment around the fire, among laughter and gestures of growing complicity, symbolized the blending of their worlds: one, the civilized king of Uruk, the other, the wild child of nature. Together, they formed an unprecedented alliance, ready to face the challenges ahead, carried by the ancient forces of the earth and blessed by the gods themselves.

***

At the dawn of the following day, Gilgamesh and Enkidou resumed their journey, swallowing another five hundred kilometers with the same ease as the day before, a distance ordinary men would have taken a month and a half to cover. Now walking side by side, they seemed to glide over the land, their united presence forming an inseparable duo, like two storms crossing the landscape in a single rush.

Alone in the vastness of the steppe, Gilgamesh lost himself in thought, anticipating the upcoming confrontation with Humbaba. As he attempted to familiarize himself with the entity they were about to face, the weight of uncertainty grew within him. Each evening, in the fading light of the sun, he implored Shamash, seeking signs and omens in his dreams that could illuminate their path and ensure their victory.

Enkidou, observing his friend's nightly routine, prepared the ground for their rest. He drew a sacred circle on the earth, within which Gilgamesh would curl up, adopting the vulnerable posture of a child in its mother's womb. In this protected space, Gilgamesh surrendered to sleep, his mind escaping to distant lands in search of visions.

Upon awakening, he shared his dreams with Enkidou, seeking in him an interpreter capable of decrypting the mysterious messages of the gods. The dream of the mountain and the rain of stones, and especially of the salvific flower in a cave, seemed to carry a message of hope and divine protection. Enkidou, listening attentively, deciphered the dream with a wisdom that was his own: the mountain represented Humbaba, the destructive anger; the flower, a symbol of Shamash, watching over them; and the cave, the unshakable heart of Gilgamesh, invulnerable to external attacks.

Reassured by this interpretation, Enkidou danced and sang, celebrating the positive nature of the dream. "Not bad, your dream, Gilgamesh. Not bad!" became their morning refrain, a litany that fortified them against the adversity to come.

Day after day, as their journey continued, Gilgamesh found comfort in the dreams sent by Shamash, and Enkidou, with his gift for interpreting them, maintained their morale. Even in the face of the most terrifying visions, Enkidou always found a way to transform anguish into assurance, assuring Gilgamesh of their inevitable success.

Thus, guided by the nocturnal omens and the wisdom of Enkidou, the two companions advanced towards their destiny, united by mutual trust and an unwavering faith in their sacred mission. Their friendship, strengthened by each trial, became the true armor protecting them against all the perils of their epic quest.

7 THE CONQUEST OF THE CEDAR FOREST

On the seventh day of their journey, they arrive at the edge of the Cedar Mountain, bearing on its back the legendary forest. Enkidu, the companion of Gilgamesh, pauses, haunted by the terrors of his childhood that resurface with piercing acuity. Gilgamesh, for his part, is seized by the majesty of the scene before him. The forest, which he had imagined as a lush oasis, reveals itself to be a dark and impenetrable mass, an ancient and wild world where lightning streaks across the sky and mist scrolls in the rhythm of storms.

'See that dark entrance, there, at the edge,' suggests Gilgamesh, captivated by the adventure that awaits them. Without further ado, they venture under the cover of the gigantic trees, entering the domain of Humbaba, the guardian of the place. The forest itself seems to awaken to their passage, reacting to the intrusion with forewarnings of its master's presence.

'Humbaba has seen us,' murmurs Enkidu, his soul heavy with ominous omens. 'He comes for us.' The air is charged with a palpable tension, and a monstrous cry echoes, confirming Enkidu's fears. Gilgamesh, though reassuring, fails to soothe his friend's apprehensions, who sees in Humbaba a force of nature unmatched, a being whose power manifests through every element of the forest.

However, Gilgamesh looks at Enkidu with deep affection, seeking to infuse courage into his wavering heart. 'Do not be overcome by fear,' he advises him, recalling the moments when Enkidu was his rock, his guide through the uncertainties of their journey. 'We are like two tumultuous rivers, and together, nothing can resist us. We will triumph.'

These words, imbued with unwavering confidence and unbreakable friendship, touch Enkidu. Despite the shadows of his past and the doubts that assail him, he rallies to Gilgamesh, ready to face the challenges of this ancient forest together. Together, they resume their march, determined to confront Humbaba and reap the fruits of their courage.

At the dawn of the seventh day, Gilgamesh and Enkidu find themselves before the Cedar Mountain, the lair of Humbaba. The heart of Enkidu, once brave in the steppe, races before the vast dark forest, a world apart where lightning streaks the sky and mists intertwine with the cries of thunder. Gilgamesh, for his part, is moved by emotion before this ancient forest he had dreamt of differently, more welcoming, but which now stands before them as a living fortress.

Without hesitation, they venture into the forest, awakening by their mere presence the legendary guardian, Humbaba. The air is charged with a palpable tension, the trees seem to move, and ancient voices whisper in the wind. The monster, toying with them, reveals itself through terrifying manifestations, explosions of earth, venomous brambles, before materializing before their eyes in a whirlwind of fire.

In the face of Gilgamesh's challenge, Houmbaba finally appears, towering, a fusion of brute strength and ancient magic. Enkidou, despite his wild past, is paralyzed with fear, but Gilgamesh, steadfast, defies the monster to measure himself against them. Encouraged by the intervention of Shamash, the sun god, and the support of his Winds, Gilgamesh engages in battle. Houmbaba, powerful but caught off guard by the coordinated attack of the elements and Gilgamesh's determination, is ultimately put at a disadvantage.

The fight is epic, a confrontation where nature itself takes sides, the trees of the forest moaning and weeping for their protector. Despite Houmbaba's initial advantage, the divine intervention of Shamash, through his Winds, unbalances the monster. Enkidou, recovering from his fall, desperately seeks to rejoin Gilgamesh, while the forces of nature unite to support the two heroes.

In a decisive moment, a heavenly gust strikes Houmbaba, inflating him with a destructive wind, while other cosmic forces disorient and weaken him. Gilgamesh, seizing this opportunity, exerts his full strength to bring down Houmbaba, marking one of the most daring feats of their joint adventure.

It's a tale of courage, friendship, and divine intervention, where man and myth converge to redefine the boundaries of the possible, and where the Cedar Forest, a silent witness, will long remember the clash between mortals and deities.

When Houmbaba falls, bringing down a hundred trees with him, the crash of his defeat echoes throughout the forest. Gilgamesh, victorious, stands over the giant's body, proclaiming the forest his own, while Enkidou, the faithful ally, immobilizes Houmbaba by placing himself on his massive chest. The forest guardian, though defeated, tries to negotiate for his life, offering the cedars in exchange for mercy, attempting to seduce the king with the promise of shared glory without shedding his blood.

But Enkidou, wary, senses deceit in Houmbaba's words and urges Gilgamesh to ignore his pleas, to recognize the malice hidden in his offers of peace. Houmbaba, in a final effort to divide the two companions, disparages Enkidou and tries to corrupt Gilgamesh's mind by promising him a friendship and greatness equivalent to what he shares with Enkidou.

Gilgamesh, however, sees through Houmbaba's ploy. He realizes that true friendship, as he has known with Enkidou, cannot be negotiated but is lived and strengthened over time through acts of loyalty and affection. Houmbaba's attempt to substitute this sincere friendship with an opportunistic alliance only strengthens Gilgamesh's resolve.

Enkidou, sensing the danger Houmbaba still poses even in defeat, insists that Gilgamesh end his life, thus eliminating the evil embodied by the forest guardian. Faced with his adversaries' determination, Houmbaba casts a final curse, predicting Enkidou's early death and misfortune for Gilgamesh. Despite this dark prophecy, the ensuing silence marks the definitive end of Houmbaba's reign over the Cedar Forest.

With the threat removed, Gilgamesh and Enkidou set about methodically destroying the cedars, marking their victory by conquering this natural treasure. After gathering enough wood to testify to their feat, they construct a raft and begin the return journey to Uruk, bearing proof of their triumph, ready to receive the acclaim of their people.

Thus, the tale of their battle against Houmbaba becomes not just a story of courage and strength but also a testament to the importance of true friendship and integrity in the face of temptation and manipulation.

8 TRIUMPH AND DEFIANCE IN URUK

Upon their return, Gilgamesh and Enkidu are welcomed by a human tide brimming with enthusiasm, gathered on the banks to celebrate the heroes' triumph. The rumor of their feat spread like lightning, attracting the curious and admirers alike, all eager to catch a glimpse of the living legends and the tangible proofs of their courage, symbolized by the majestic cedars that fragranced the air of the harbor. In the tumult, some are splashed by the tumultuous waters of the Euphrates, while others, more daring, venture on makeshift rafts to get closer to the victors and their treasure.

The victory transforms Uruk into a theater of rejoicing. Gilgamesh, in an act of royal generosity, orders the opening of the storehouses and the liberal distribution of the city's riches: grains, fruits, oils, and an abundance of beer and wine to quench the thirst of a jubilant population. The city gives itself over to celebration, the most exquisite dishes circulate freely, and pure happiness permeates the air.

The temples, at the heart of this effervescence, become places of sacrifice and gratitude like never before. The faithful crowd the altars of Anu, Ishtar, and especially Shamash, the sun god who guided and protected Gilgamesh and Enkidu on their perilous quest. Their prayers, mixed with the sacred smoke and the symphony of religious hymns, rise to the heavens, forming a fragrant veil of thanksgiving that envelops the city.

On that day, Uruk transforms into a living ode to the greatness of its heroes and the benevolence of the gods, a dazzling manifestation of the symbiosis between the divine and the human. In this collective jubilation, Gilgamesh and Enkidu are celebrated not only as victorious warriors but also as catalysts for a moment of unity and deeply human sharing, testifying to the power and generosity of the human spirit, capable of transforming personal glory into a collective celebration of life and community.

As the celebration is in full swing within the palace walls, Enkidu becomes the center of attention, passionately recounting their heroic quest. With a beer in hand, he shares their journey, his gestures animating each story, bringing to life the dark forest, his own fears, the titanic clashes, and the capricious winds that accompanied them. Enkidu, through his tales, transports his audience to the heart of the adventure, feeling again the intensity of each moment. His mind occasionally wanders into the memories of the forest, reliving his confrontation with Humbaba and realizing how much he has changed, how much he has overcome his fears through the unwavering friendship of Gilgamesh.

Meanwhile, Gilgamesh, desiring a moment of solitude, moves away from the festivities to meditate on their feat. Immersed in an aromatic bath, he lets his mind drift towards the wild expanses of the steppe, reflecting on the lessons learned alongside Enkidu, and the constant support of Shamash throughout their quest. Alone in the cooled garden of the palace, he expresses his gratitude to Shamash, the god who has always supported him.

Suddenly, a teasing female voice breaks his reflection. Gilgamesh, wary, soon recognizes Ishtar, the dazzling goddess of love and war, who, in a seductive play, manifests in all her splendor. Ishtar, charmed by the exploits narrated by Enkidu, attempts to seduce Gilgamesh, offering him a marriage full of promises. But Gilgamesh, aware of Ishtar's past unhappy lovers, rebuffs her advances with disdain, listing the betrayals and misfortunes she inflicted on her former loves.

Their confrontation reaches its climax when Ishtar, furious at being rejected, hurls curses at Gilgamesh before disappearing, leaving behind an atmosphere charged with tension and defiance. Gilgamesh, though victorious in this verbal joust, anticipates with dark concern the repercussions of this affront to such a powerful goddess.

Ishtar, attempting to snuggle up to Gilgamesh in a desperate quest for affection, is met with his icy indifference. As she lists the rewards she offers him in marriage, Gilgamesh, unflappable, poses a question dripping with sarcasm about the cost of these gifts. In a fit of anger, Ishtar throws her cup at him and slashes his skin with divine fury, but Gilgamesh, dodging the assault, immobilizes the goddess with a firm grip, flipping her onto the damp ground.

Under his hold, he speaks with contempt of Ishtar's previous lovers, each betrayed and transformed by her cruel whims. From Tammuz, the fallen lover, to the hunted lion, Gilgamesh recounts the fates broken by Ishtar, cynically asking her what end she has in store for him. Ishtar, furious, struggles in vain, her face distorted by rage, makeup streaming down in dark rivulets.

Gilgamesh, pushing Ishtar away with disdain, rejects her advances and challenges her to reveal her true intentions. Standing up, straightening his garments, Ishtar vanishes in a whirlwind of anger, leaving behind a veiled threat of vengeance. Gilgamesh, for his part, remains alone, pondering the storm he has just provoked, aware of the future repercussions of this bold refusal.

9 DIVINE WRATH AND MORTAL TRIUMPH

Ishtar, burning with anger and indignation, does not seek the comfort of her own sanctuary but rushes towards Anu, the divine ruler, carrying her grievances. Anu, anticipating the storm that Ishtar's visit represents, braces himself to face the tempest of her fury. Without mincing words, Ishtar launches her complaints like arrows, accusing Anu of indifference in the face of Gilgamesh's insolence. Anu, wise but weary, listens to his daughter's lamentations with worn patience, aware of the challenges posed by her impetuous temperament.

The conversation quickly becomes heated, with Ishtar presenting Anu with a dilemma: to intervene or let chaos reign on earth. She demands the Bull of Heaven, a mythical creature, as an instrument of her revenge. Faced with Ishtar's threat to unleash the dead and reverse the natural order, Anu weighs his options with heavy reluctance. The goddess, manipulative and determined, pressures her father, reminding him of the disastrous consequences of his refusal.

Finally, Anu, in a gesture of weary concession, grants Ishtar's request. He plunges his hand into the cosmos, searching for the sleeping Bull of Heaven among the stars. With a titanic effort, he draws the creature towards the world of mortals, marking the beginning of a devastating trial for Gilgamesh and his people. The sky itself trembles at the roar of the Bull, announcing an impending divine showdown.

Uruk is suddenly shaken by a seismic wave, startling its inhabitants awake. The absence of clouds hints at a mystery, leaving the city in anxious anticipation. The calm is short-lived; a second, more powerful shockwave shakes the city's foundations, raising fears of divine wrath. Anxious whispers run through the streets, fueled by the sudden appearance of a devouring chasm in the potter's district, swallowing homes and lives indiscriminately.

The catastrophe spreads, striking at the heart of the districts, leaving Uruk disfigured by the disappearance of its inhabitants and structures. Gilgamesh and Enkidu, witnessing this devastation, sense the origin of this scourge. As the earth itself seems to cry out their names, a gaping chasm forms, threatening to swallow Enkidu. By a miraculous escape, he avoids death, finding himself face to face with the terrifying manifestation of their challenge: the Bull of Heaven.

Emerging from the abyss like a mountain in fury, the Bull stands, a monolith of power and divine anger, its appearance marking the city with an ominous omen. The roar of the Bull, laden with deadly threat, echoes through Uruk, announcing the beginning of an epic confrontation.

Gilgamesh, facing this embodied threat, grasps the magnitude of the challenge posed by Ishtar, their fate intertwined with that of the wrathful deity. The city, hanging on this moment of truth, holds its breath as its two heroes prepare to confront the celestial scourge, aware of the impact of their fight not only on their own destiny but also on the future of Uruk.

— "This is the work of Ishtar!" Gilgamesh exclaims, turning to Enkidu, his determination as sharp as his drawn sword.

— "She will find no favor in our eyes!" he proclaims, as they charge together towards the embodied threat.

The Bull of Heaven, a titan among beasts, does not wait to be provoked to reveal its primordial fury. Its charge is an earthquake, a challenge thrown not only to the two heroes but also to the very order of the city. Their clash, a collision of wills, shakes the heart of Uruk, casting Gilgamesh and Enkidu into a whirlwind of dust and blood. The outcome seems sealed by the brute power of the divine creature.

Yet, cunning unfolds in the minds of the warriors. To flee, not as a sign of defeat, but to better trap their adversary in the city's labyrinth, where its brute force could be turned against it. The Bull, in its relentless pursuit, finds itself caught in the game of human strategy, each step taking it further from victory and closer to its fall.

The deadlock turns out to be the final theater of this struggle, a trap where Gilgamesh, in a bold move, awaits the beast's charge. Enkidu, from his urban vantage point, dives at the crucial moment to hinder the embodied fury, seizing its tail in a superhuman effort.

The turnaround is brutal. Gilgamesh, seizing the moment of vulnerability, plunges under the massive bulk of the animal and, with a precise and desperate blow, delivers the fatal thrust. The defeat of the Bull is a tragic symphony, a mix of rage and resignation, as its blood, like an end river, traces its path in the dust of Uruk's streets.

In its last breath, the Bull of Heaven fixes its victors with a shadow of understanding in its dying gaze. Its final roar is a farewell, an acknowledgment that, despite its divine strength, it succumbs to the weight of mortality. The gods, witnesses to this fall, are reminded of the tenacity and audacity of men.

Gilgamesh and Enkidu, through their victory, triumph not only over a mythical creature; they reaffirm the power of humanity against the immutable, a challenge thrown to the stars themselves.

Scarcely has the breath of the Bull of Heaven extinguished than another concert rises, a symphony of pain and fury. Ishtar, the fallen goddess, stands there, on the terrace of her sanctuary, surrounded by her mourning followers, weeping over the loss of her divine champion. Gilgamesh's anger bursts like a storm against her, his name thundering in the air with unprecedented force. Without a moment's hesitation, they seize the corpse of the Bull, a symbol of their triumph and Ishtar's defeat, and drag it before her as a macabre offering.

"Here is your champion, Ishtar! See what has become of him by our hand!" Gilgamesh's challenge resonates, as the sight of the felled beast triggers a storm of violent emotions among Ishtar's servants, their bodies wracked with spasms of anger and despair. In a gesture of ultimate provocation, Enkidu tears off a thigh of the Bull and flings it disdainfully towards the goddess, sowing terror among the divine.

The priestesses, horrified, vanish into the shadow of their temple, while Gilgamesh, exultant in their victory, defies Ishtar one last time with boundless audacity. "Had you been at our mercy, Ishtar, it is you who would lie in the dust!"

Carried by the cheers of a jubilant crowd, Gilgamesh and Enkidu make their way through Uruk, hailed as liberating heroes. Their legend, already grandiose, is further enriched: victors over Humbaba and destroyers of the Cedar Forest, they have now felled the Bull of Heaven itself. "They are invincible! Glory to Gilgamesh and to Enkidu, his faithful companion!"

In a quest for purification, the two warriors head towards the Euphrates, whose welcoming waters promise to wash away the ardor and madness that drive them. They plunge into the river, leaving behind the echoes of their feats, confident that the current will carry away the fury and pain, mixing them with the salty waters of the distant sea.

10 THE END OF ENKIDU

In the shadow of the purifying waters of the Euphrates, a dark fate is woven, impervious to the mercy of the current. The gods, stirred by the turmoil caused by Ishtar, convene in council to judge the actions of the daring mortals. Anu, the celestial sovereign, deceived by Ishtar's machinations, is hesitant to take sides, opting for the most neutral solution: the equal condemnation of both companions, Gilgamesh and Enkidu, proposing an outcome as radical as it is unjust.

Enlil, the voice of reason tempered by authority, rises to contest this blind equity. He distinguishes between the demigod Gilgamesh, a reflection of the divine, and Enkidu, the earthly emanation shaped from clay and water, arguing that the extinction of Enkidu would bear less consequence, a divine experiment interrupted, while the fall of Gilgamesh would shake the very foundations of their own essence.

Shamash, the illuminator of the heavens, then brings his light to the debate, reminding of his own involvement in the terrestrial exploits of the duo. His bold defense sends a shockwave through the divine assembly, raising the question of his own guilt and the relative innocence of Enkidu in this celestial affair.

In this divine tumult, Ea, the wise among the gods, proposes a resolution that attempts to reconcile all perspectives. He acknowledges the greatness of Enkidu, this being molded who transcended his initial nature to reach a heroic stature, and suggests that his end would not only be an appropriate conclusion to his narrative arc but also the ultimate trial for Gilgamesh. The challenge is no longer to triumph on the battlefield but to face loss and mourning.

Ea's proposal, imbued with wisdom and cruelty, promises to subject Gilgamesh to an unprecedented trial, that of human suffering in the face of the inevitable death of a loved one. Enkidu, whose existence has been a series of victories and revelations, is assigned a tragic role in this final act, his demise becoming the catalyst for Gilgamesh's greatest challenge: to confront the fragility of the human condition and the finiteness of existence.

***

Enkidu, the warrior molded from the earth and divine will, is struck by a nocturnal vision, an ominous omen delivered by the gods themselves. Startled awake by the weight of this revelation, he is overtaken by a fever that consumes his strength, marking the beginning of his slow decline. In a gesture of despair, he implores the heavens, hoping his prayer, like smoke, disperses and carries away the curse consuming him.

Faced with the inevitable, Enkidu shares his distress with Gilgamesh, his brother-in-arms, his soulmate in greatness and tragedy. Gilgamesh, refusing to accept the grim omen, counters fate with an unwavering faith in life. He urges Enkidu to fight the illness as they have faced the most formidable opponents together, to not give in to the despair that paves the way to death.

Thus begins their ultimate quest, not for glory, but for survival. Together, they traverse sacred places, pleading for the gods' mercy, seeking remedy from the healing goddess and sages with ancestral knowledge. Gilgamesh, driven by love and determination, guides Enkidu through rituals and treatments, hoping to thwart fate.

But the disease is a more relentless enemy than the monsters they've defeated. It creeps deeper into Enkidu's body, making him falter like a reed in the storm, until it pins him to his bed, a shadow of the invincible warrior he once was. One night, in a fit of delirium, Enkidu attempts to flee his ailment, to escape from this prison of pain, but collapses, defeated, perhaps without even a cry, in the darkness of his room, where even Gilgamesh cannot follow.

This desperate struggle against the illness becomes the theater of a more intimate battle, that of the spirit against the body, of will against fate, a fight where victory is nothing more than each breath wrested from the grasp of death. And for Gilgamesh, it marks the beginning of a journey of pain and reflection, a voyage that will take him to the boundaries of the human and the divine, in search of an answer to the why of suffering and finiteness.

In the royal palace of Uruk, a feverish agitation is felt as servants rush, bringing fresh water and linens, to try to soothe Enkidu's suffering. Doctors crowd at his bedside, desperately seeking a cure for his mysterious ailment, while Gilgamesh, his brother-in-arms, rushes to support him. With trembling tenderness, he implores Enkidu to lie down, to not waste his last strength in a futile fight against the invisible enemy assaulting him.

Enkidu, his eyes filled with a distant glow, murmurs words evocative of the steppe, that wild and free space where he once reigned supreme. He longs to return, to merge one last time with the land of his birth, far from the confining walls of the palace, far from the disease consuming him. He dreams of being scattered by the wind, of nourishing the gazelles he so loved, of becoming dust under their light hooves.

Gilgamesh, faced with his friend's distress, promises to fulfill his last wish, to take his spirit, or whatever remains of it, back to the steppe, to the very place where their friendship was forged. He even considers building a chariot to transport Enkidu without the slightest harm, a final tribute to their unbreakable brotherhood. But for that, Enkidu must hold on, gather his strength for the final journey.

As night falls, death silently approaches Enkidu, drawing him towards the realm of shadows. He passes through the gates of the Dark Land, guided by funeral torches, until a terrifying demon seizes him, marking him with its deadly seal. In this dark and desolate beyond, he recognizes faces once powerful, now reduced to eternal wandering, forgotten souls condemned to feed on humus and mud.

The revelation of this oblivion as a second death spurs Enkidu to a final effort, a desperate wish projected towards Gilgamesh: not to be forgotten. As his life force fades, the queen of the Underworld, Ereshkigal, takes hold of the tablet of his fate, destroying it with a gesture, thus sealing his demise.

Gilgamesh, at his bedside, can only contemplate the void left by his friend's absence, inwardly promising to carry his memory, to defy oblivion, to immortalize Enkidu in tales and hearts, so that his name never fades into the sands of time.

11 After the Funeral: Gilgamesh's Quest for

Immortality

Gilgamesh is roused from his sleep by a ghostly rustling, his heart leaping at the thought that Enkidu might be calling out from the confines of his bed of pain. In a burst of despair, he whispers his friend's name, hoping against hope that it's a terrifying nightmare where Enkidu, transformed into a bird trapped in darkness, struggles to catch his attention. Gilgamesh apologizes, believing himself guilty of a moment of inattention, but finds Enkidu in eternal silence, his spirit having already taken flight to the unknown.

The brutal reality hits Gilgamesh when he realizes the lack of response, life having left his companion's body. In a gesture mixing gentleness and despair, he tries to awaken Enkidu, to bring him back to life with his shaking, but the inert body falls back, heavy with the absence of its soul. Gilgamesh, facing this irreversible loss, unleashes his pain and incomprehension. He reproaches Enkidu for his solitary departure, having always faced adversities shoulder to shoulder. Why, he wonders, did Enkidu choose to leave without him, without their unbreakable brotherhood to fight this last enemy?

Wrapped in a desperate embrace, Gilgamesh talks to Enkidu as if he could still hear him, promising to never forget him, to carry their friendship beyond valleys and mountains, into the vastness of the steppe that saw them grow together. He evokes the gazelles, symbols of their wild and free past, in an attempt to recall Enkidu to life, to convince him to return for one last hunt under the starry sky.

But his words find no echo but the silence of the room, his promises floating in the air, powerless to reanimate his friend's soul. Gilgamesh, heartbroken, swears to keep Enkidu's memory alive, to celebrate him through songs and stories, so that never will the wind erase his name from the annals of time. In his sorrow, he finds new determination: to confront the inevitability of death and seek, perhaps, an answer to the enigma of existence.

In the silence of the room where Enkidu rests, Gilgamesh is overwhelmed by immeasurable grief. In a heart-wrenching monologue, he promises his departed friend to eternally engrave him in the memory of the world. Statues in his likeness, fashioned from noble and imperishable materials, will adorn the kingdom's entrances, standing as sentinels over the land Enkidu so loved. Gilgamesh commits to having the epic of their friendship transcribed by his scribes, so that Enkidu's story may be perpetuated through the ages, an endless tale that will travel beyond lands and eras.

He assures Enkidu that his spirit will continue to inspire the daily life of his people. At dawn, when the mist rises, they will see Enkidu's breath; in the rustling of the barley under the sun, they will feel his joy; and at dusk, around the campfires, they will honor the silence of his reveries. In this poignant farewell, Gilgamesh expresses boundless love and devotion for his friend, his heart heavy with the acceptance of his loss.

When the palace servants come for news, they find their king in a funereal embrace with his companion, a tableau of sorrow and fidelity that leaves them speechless with sadness. The news of Enkidu's death spreads quickly throughout the city, plunging Uruk into collective mourning, a sea of red garments symbolizing the depth of the shared grief.

Enkidu's funeral is held the next day, a ceremony that reflects his life between two worlds: the wild expanses of the steppe and the paved streets of the city. Gilgamesh, in a final gesture of affection, places a gazelle horn in his friend's hands, a symbol of their shared past, a bridge between life and death.

***

After the funeral, Gilgamesh is faced with absolute solitude. Despite the physical presence of Enkidu in memories and monuments, his absence is an abyss that nothing can fill. Gilgamesh wanders through the corridors of the palace, talking to the shadow of his friend, vainly hoping for a sign, a whisper, any manifestation of his presence. But the walls remain silent, impenetrable, returning Gilgamesh to his solitude and despair, a king haunted by the specter of his lost friend.

Gilgamesh, heart heavy with sorrow, enters Enkidu's now-empty room, hoping to find a remnant of his presence. The reality of his absence hits him fully, deepening the chasm of his loneliness even more. In a corner of the room, an ancient chest catches his attention. Opening it, he is overwhelmed by a flood of emotions, for inside lies a collection of intimate items belonging to Enkidu, each piece evoking a vivid memory of their unbreakable friendship. This treasure is the tangible memory of Enkidu, a fragile but precious link to the lost friend.

Gilgamesh, kneeling, loses himself in the contemplation of these relics. For a moment, the figure of Enkidu seems to come to life in its fullness, evoking their shared past, their adventures, their bond. But this apparition vanishes as soon as Gilgamesh tries to grasp it, leaving behind an even deeper void.

Desperate, Gilgamesh leaves the city of Uruk, seeking in the vastness of the steppe an answer to his unbearable grief. Nature, a silent witness to his quest, imposes its rhythm, its indifference, forcing him to confront his solitude and dismay. He wanders aimlessly, subsisting on the little the earth is willing to offer him, becoming almost one with the wild landscape, yet finding no comfort.

Then, just when Gilgamesh seems to have lost all hope, the steppe offers him a vision of Enkidu, not as the valiant companion of happy days, but as the shadow of the man he was, marked by defeat and death. This terrifying apparition is a turning point for Gilgamesh. The reality of death seizes him, not only as an external loss but as an intimate and personal threat.

In a cry of rebellion against his mortal fate, Gilgamesh vows to find Utnapishtim, the immortal, to conquer or beg for the secret of eternity. Armed for a new quest, he seeks the blessing of Shamash before venturing beyond the known world, driven by the desperate desire to thwart death itself.

Thus begins the most audacious journey of Gilgamesh, no longer in search of glory or adventure, but for an answer to humanity's oldest enigma: how to escape the finality of death?

12 Gilgamesh's Final Journey

Thus, Gilgamesh sets off, carried by a quest that transcends him, whispering scattered words about the battle to be waged at the ends of the world, about eternity to be snatched away like a trophy. Uruk, his city, is troubled by his hasty departure, murmuring about the madness that seems to guide him since the loss of Enkidou. But Gilgamesh, his mind entirely on his purpose, no longer perceives the concerns of his city. He disappears into the distance, leaving behind him a trail of dust soon dissipated by the scorching breath of the plains.

Directed towards the East, where the sun begins its course, Gilgamesh defies the falling night to measure himself against the mountains, crossing with tireless fervor each peak that hides another, in search of a clear horizon, a sign to guide his path.

The journey continues, marked by exhausting ascents, provoked avalanches, overcome rockfalls. Gilgamesh surrenders to a march that has become as vital, as involuntary as the beating of his heart. And when, at the end of a full lunar cycle, exhaustion brings him down in a clearing perfumed with the cool night, he collapses, unaware of the lurking danger.

Then, a creature of the night, drawn by his vulnerability, approaches. Gilgamesh, torn from sleep by a sharp pain, grabs his sword, and in a desperate burst, engages in a fierce battle against his assailant. Blows rain down, growls mix with the fury of the confrontation, until, exhausted, both fighters collapse, letting the clearing catch its breath.

At dawn, Gilgamesh discovers the extent of his feat: he has defeated a bear with formidable natural weapons. This first substantial meal in a long time reminds him of Enkidu, his brother-in-arms, and in a gesture of communion with his memory, he celebrates their indomitable spirit.

Reinvigorated, clad in the hide of the bear he has just slain, Gilgamesh resumes his journey, determination embedded in his being, each step bringing him closer to his dream of immortality, each trial binding him more tightly to the indomitable spirit of Enkidu.

As Gilgamesh progresses, with each waning moon, he is transformed, his human essence evaporating to make way for a brute force that relentlessly drives him forward. His body becomes lean, almost spectral, a framework of muscle and bone wrapped in skin marked by the trials of the journey. No one, seeing him thus draped in bear skin, hair wild adorned with debris of nature, could recognize the once resplendent king of Uruk.

He has become a creature of the quest, driven solely by the memory of Enkidu and the terror of his own end.

Through mountains and adversities, he fights, at times reminiscent of Enkidu's early days, wild and untamed. Confrontations with the beasts and strange beings that inhabit these heights only strengthen his resolve, each victory and each loss distancing him further from humanity, drawing him towards something more primal.

And then, there is the endless plain and, beyond, the Twin Mountains, dark and majestic, guardians of an ancient secret. It is there, between these stone colossi, that the passage to Gilgamesh's ultimate goal stands.

His cry of triumph echoes, filled with raw assurance, but he does not account for the guardians of this threshold, the Scorpion-Men, who observe him with a curiosity mingled with mistrust.

Faced with these sentinels, Gilgamesh prepares for battle, his survival instinct overriding fatigue and accumulated injuries. They scrutinize him, recognizing not just any mortal, but a being marked by the gods, wrapped in an aura that betrays his exceptional nature.

A tense dialogue ensues between the fallen king and these legendary creatures. Despite the palpable hostility, mutual recognition is established. Gilgamesh, armed with his unwavering determination, reveals his identity and purpose, seeking to convince the Scorpion-Men to let him pass.

The revelation of his quest awakens in these guardians a curiosity tinged with respect. Gilgamesh, even on the brink of exhaustion, embodies a will that defies the limits of the known world. The sentinels, faced with the king's obstinacy, are confronted with a choice: to block the path of this unique man or grant him access to this mythical passage, where every step is a trial, every thought a battle against oneself.

Gilgamesh, facing this ultimate challenge, does not waver. His bow ready, he defies the darkness ahead, prepared to face the hundred thousand steps and thoughts that still separate him from his ultimate confrontation with fate.

Faced with the defiance of the Scorpion-Men, Gilgamesh stands ready, bow drawn, anticipating the confrontation. The tension is palpable in the air, a dangerous dance where every movement counts. The guardians, all armor and venom, opt for cunning rather than brute force, perhaps recognizing in this man, torn by trials, an indomitable will.

"We are here only to watch," announces the male, his voice grating like sand under a blade. "Approach without fear."

"Never has a man trod this ground," murmurs the female, her gaze fixed on Gilgamesh. "Who are you then, to brave what no other has dared?"

"I am Gilgamesh," he replies, breath short, bow ready to release its death.

A heavy silence settles as the Scorpion-Men consider this intruder, this once-powerful king, now reduced to a shadow of himself by his relentless quest.

Why this path? Why this quest?" the male asks, glancing towards the Twin Mountains that stand as guardians of an ancient secret.

"To find Utnapishtim, to understand the mystery of life and death, to escape the oblivion that swallowed Enkidu, my brother-in-arms, my soulmate."

Faced with Gilgamesh's determination, the sentinels step aside, revealing the narrow passage that snakes between the mountains, a path wrapped in shadows and whispers, promising revelations or perdition.

"Remember," the male says mockingly, "the challenge is great: one hundred thousand steps in the dark, accompanied by your darkest thoughts."

The female, in a final provocative gesture, offers a quick exit, her stinger glowing with deadly venom. But Gilgamesh, unshakeable, refuses the easy way out, refuses the fate others seek to impose on him.

With renewed resolve, he plunges into the passage, leaving behind the guardians astounded by his tenacity. The echo of his steps intertwines with the distant cries of the Scorpion-Men:

"Do not forget, Gilgamesh, one hundred thousand steps, one hundred thousand thoughts. May your will illuminate your path."

Thus, armed with nothing but his determination, Gilgamesh

advances into the unknown, each step a challenge to death, each thought a battle for life.

13 Gilgamesh's Path to Redemption

As soon as he enters the dark corridor, Gilgamesh is struck by an invisible force that violently propels him against the rocky wall. Isolated in the darkness, he desperately tries to pierce the veil of obscurity, to discern his assailant, but in vain. A second assault, even more brutal, hits him squarely, a blow felt as a javelin piercing his heart. He screams, in pain, in defiance, calling his enemy to reveal itself.

A fetid breath fills the space, carrying with it the rumbling voice of the abyss, a presence both immaterial and oppressive. Gilgamesh recognizes in this tumult the ghost of the Bull he once defeated before the temple of Ishtar, an apparition that charges again, relentless, unstoppable.

Defeated, he falls to his knees, hands pressed against his chest searching for a nonexistent wound, thus uncovering the illusion of his adversary. Yet, the pain is palpable, real, a suffering embodied by the memory of past battles, of victories and losses.

Silence returns, heavy, laden with deceptive calm. Gilgamesh finds himself facing his own demons, confronted with the violence of his actions, the brutality of his choices. Houmbaba, in a final echo of rage, reflects back the echo of his own deeds, a painful resonance of his own fury.

"One hundred thousand steps in the darkness... One hundred thousand thoughts..." This corridor, this challenge, becomes the mirror of his existence, each step a confrontation with himself, each breath a battle to accept what he has been, to hope for what he might become.

In this moment of distress, a revelation: to accept. To accept the weight of his past, the heaviness of his faults. This dark path transforms into a road to redemption, a quest not only for eternal life but for a deep understanding of oneself.

Thus, Gilgamesh, the once invincible warrior, moves forward, shaken but resolved, through the labyrinth of his own shadows, each step a trial, each thought a stone on the path to his redemption.

The piercing cries of the felled cedars assault Gilgamesh, each sound striking his mind like painful arrows. He is overwhelmed by the memory of ancient trees falling under the force of his blows, their essence lamenting under the assault of steel. Confronted with the destruction he has sown in the Cedar Forest, he accepts the suffering he inflicted, ingesting the weight of his past actions.

A macabre procession of memories then parades, marching through the darkness of his mind: conquered realms, devastated cities, peoples enslaved by his hand. Each battle, each triumph once celebrated, transforms into a burden of remorse and pain.

"One hundred thousand steps in the darkness... One hundred thousand reflections..."

Gilgamesh is assailed by the entirety of his misdeeds, each trial inviting him to reap the bitter fruit of his violence. He is forced to endure the pain he caused, to weep for the blood he spilled, to suffer for every tear he made flow.

Deep within himself, a word forms, a concept until now unexpressed due to its gravity and scope. Despite the pauses overwhelmed by despair, despite the silent calls to Shamash, his divine protector, no light comes to pierce the darkness enveloping him.

Bearing the crushing weight of his guilt, Gilgamesh advances, struggling against the mountain he seems to drag behind him. It is no longer just the burden of his own existence he carries, but the very mass of the mountain, and that unspoken word swirling in his heart, pushing him to the brink of exhaustion.

Suddenly, a faint light appears in the distance, a promise of an exit or a cruel illusion? The walls of the passageway narrow, as if to guide him, to encourage him. Hope is reborn, although the light seems too good to be true.

In a desperate effort, Gilgamesh crawls towards this promise of salvation, pushed by the mountain itself. Freedom is within reach. Gathering his last reserves of energy, he propels himself forward, and the mountain finally releases him from its oppressive grip.

As the darkness gives way to clarity and fresh air caresses his face, the word he has held back finally escapes his lips, a whisper that seals his journey through the darkness:

— Forgiveness...

***

Gilgamesh emerges into a clearing bathed in a mysterious light, a light that warms without burning, gently caressing every fiber of his exhausted being. He finds unexpected comfort, as if each ray was a soothing balm on his deep wounds. Amazed, he discovers he rests at the heart of a unique orchard, where the trees are adorned not with ordinary fruits, but with glittering jewels that play with the light, diffracting it into a thousand calming colors.

Unable to resist the urge to explore this enchanting place, Gilgamesh rises, guided by renewed curiosity. He wanders from tree to tree, each offering a different variety of precious stones, their colors and brightness competing in beauty. Garnets whisper ancient secrets, agates laugh softly, amber pours its golden light like a benevolent rain on Gilgamesh, transforming him, purifying him.

This garden, this sanctuary of gemstones, speaks to him in a way he cannot ignore. Long-buried memories resurface, forgotten friendly faces smile at him through the prism of the gems. A feeling of familiarity overwhelms him, a deep resonance with this place that seems to welcome and recognize him.

Faced with this enigma, a familiar voice rises: that of Shamash, his protector, who urges him to understand, to accept the truth unfolding before him. Guided by this reassuring presence, Gilgamesh engages in introspection, realizing that this marvelous garden is himself in his purest form, unaltered by the trials and errors of his tumultuous life.

Excited by this revelation, he ponders eternal life, the goal that has pushed him here, on this desperate quest against death and oblivion. But Shamash's response is delayed, plunging Gilgamesh into a meaningful silence. In this silence, Gilgamesh understands that his journey is far from over, that the quest for immortality may be a mirage, another trial on his path towards wisdom and redemption.

Doubt and disappointment momentarily darken the idyllic landscape, reminding him that despite revelations and inner transformations, the struggle to understand the true meaning of his life, to accept his mortality and find peace, is far from finished.

14 Crossing the Waters of Redemption

Gilgamesh, unsatisfied and driven by an unquenchable thirst to conquer not just a garden but the entirety of the earth that supports it, seals his inner treasures once more and launches into a new frenzy of travel. A few days later, his steps lead him to the edge of a vast and shimmering expanse: the sea, a liquid frontier that embraces the ends of the known world, unfolds majestically before him. Kneeling before this immensity, Gilgamesh marvels at the peaceful beauty of the shore, the ceaseless dialogue between the waves and the sand, and thinks that he has reached the outermost limits of the land inhabited by mortals.

Before him, the horizon merges with the sky in a dance of light and saltwater, while a natural barrier of rocks awakens in him a powerful intuition: it is there, beyond this natural border, that he must seek Utnapishtim, the man who defied death. Filled with new certainty, Gilgamesh rushes towards this direction, his heart pounding at the thought of the imminent discovery.

But as he approaches, the illusion dissipates to reveal a scene all too terrestrial: a modest hut made of sun-dried bricks, not a palace of immortality, but a humble refuge against the vastness of the sea. Gilgamesh observes the signs of a simple life, jars lined up, a beer vat, a woman going about her daily chores, and realizes his mistake. What he had taken for a sanctuary of eternity is but a tavern, a place of passage for travelers of this ephemeral world.

Consumed by frustration and anger at this new failure, at what he perceives as mockery by the gods, Gilgamesh is swept up in an internal storm that reflects in his furious assault towards the tavern. The proprietor, witnessing this unleashed force that seems to herald her own end, flees terrified to take refuge behind the walls of her establishment, barricading the door behind her.

In this desperate quest, where each discovery seems to be just another illusion on the obstacle-laden path to immortality, Gilgamesh confronts not only the limits of the physical world but also his own limits, the fragility of his hopes, and the harsh reality of the human condition.

But here Gilgamesh stands at the door, his anger making the wood tremble under his furious knocks. Siduri's simple building, the tavern keeper, seems frail against his rage. Aware that her fate is in the hands of the gods and that her only escape is to accept what life imposes on her, Siduri finds within herself the courage to open the door. Before her stands a disheveled figure, whose wild appearance and burning gaze betray a long journey and a desperate quest.

Siduri, despite her initial fright at the sight of this man with a face haunted by shadows, cannot help but perceive behind his threatening facade, the depth of despair. She offers him the hospitality of her home, hands him a jug of beer from which he drinks with a thirst that goes beyond the simple quest for refreshment. Sitting in the shadow of the tavern, the aromas of the brew seem to revive in him memories of a previous life, an existence where sweetness and friendship were not chimeras.

Touched by the loneliness emanating from this broken man, Siduri invites him to confide, kneels before him, and takes his hand in a gesture of compassion. Under the soothing influence of the tavern keeper, Gilgamesh finally lets the words that have weighed on his soul for too long escape.

He speaks of Enkidu, the wild friend, the lost friend, who became the axis around which his entire existence revolved. With Enkidu, he faced insurmountable challenges, tasted the glory of impossible victories, touched immortality through their joint exploits. But behind the story of these extraordinary adventures, it's the void left by Enkidu's death that shines through, a void that neither glory nor power can fill. In Siduri's gaze, Gilgamesh seeks a reflection of understanding, a sign that his quest for meaning, his desire to transcend the death of his friend and his own, are not in vain.

Before Siduri, the tavern keeper, Gilgamesh stands, his mind tormented by his own revelations. The tale of his adventures and his desperate quest to escape the fate of death leaves Siduri moved. She gently strokes Gilgamesh's damaged hand, her words striving to pierce the armor of pain that encloses him. "Abandon this futile quest, Gilgamesh," she whispers, "eternal life is a mirage, a promise that even the gods cannot keep. All that is earthly is ephemeral. Find peace in the present moment, in the simple joy of being alive, before the hail of life ravages your inner garden."

Siduri, with her soft words and calm wisdom, offers Gilgamesh an escape, a chance to reconcile with his humanity. She proposes to give back what the quest has taken from him: the ability to love, to touch, to fully feel the life flowing in his veins, far from the senseless quest for immortality.

But the shadow of Enkidu still looms over Gilgamesh, leading him to wonder if this encounter is not another trap on his path. Suspicion gnaws at him: is this a new trial by the gods, eager to divert him from his ultimate goal? His heart wrestles between the desire to stay and the need to continue his quest until the call of the unknown pushes him to stand up, animated by an unshakable resolution.

Siduri then reveals to him that Utnapishtim is located across the vast expanse of water, a realm no one has ever managed to reach. Gilgamesh, determined, is not discouraged and sets off in search of Urshanabi, the ferryman, the only one capable of taking him to his destination.

In the forest, the confrontation with the Stone-Beings, guardians of the ferryman, results in a field of debris. Gilgamesh then realizes the magnitude of his mistake: by destroying these creatures, he has annihilated his only means of crossing the Waters of Death. Urshanabi, a horrified witness to this destruction, is forced to admit the impossibility of their passage.

Thus, by the sea, Gilgamesh stands facing the infinity of the waters, his path to immortality blocked by the consequences of his own actions. The quest now seems more elusive than ever, leaving the king of Uruk facing the most bitter truth: even for the greatest of heroes, some boundaries remain insurmountable.

Gilgamesh, faced with failure and despair, sits defeated before the vastness of the sea. The bitter realization of his rash actions, which have ruined his last chance of crossing to the land of immortality, weighs heavily on him. However, the unexpected compassion of Urshanabi, the ferryman, offers him a glimmer of hope.

Urshanabi, moved by Gilgamesh's desperate quest and deep sadness, approaches with a bold proposition, a last resort to reach the other shore. Although the task seems superhuman, the idea of cutting down one hundred and twenty massive trees into fire-hardened oars ignites a spark in Gilgamesh's eyes. This act of unexpected generosity, despite the destruction caused by Gilgamesh, awakens in him a sense of gratitude and humility.

Gilgamesh, with tears in his eyes, realizes the greatness of Urshanabi's soul. In a renewed surge of determination, he stands up, ready to take on this new challenge. Urshanabi's offer is not just a simple gesture of help; it's a bridge to redemption for Gilgamesh, a chance to atone for his past mistakes through effort and sacrifice.

With a resolution strengthened by hope and the budding friendship with the ferryman, Gilgamesh accepts the challenge. The Herculean task of preparing the ferry for the dangerous crossing now stands before him, no longer as an impossibility but as a path to the fulfillment of his quest. With renewed strength and unwavering faith in the possibility of changing his fate, Gilgamesh embarks on the preparation, ready to face the uncertainty of the future with courage and determination.

15 The Search for Eternal Wisdom

In a burst of fierce determination, Gilgamesh tackles the Herculean task of felling one hundred and twenty gigantic trees. With meticulous care, he strips them of their branches, carves them, hardens them with fire, then loads them onto the ferry. Urshanabi, the ferryman, without wasting a moment, raises the sail, ready to face the open sea. The wind, complicit in their haste, carries them with surprising vigor, allowing them to accomplish in three days a journey that would normally have taken a month and a half.

Suddenly, the breeze calms, the sea stills, and a thick fog rises like a wall before them. It's the heralding sign of the dreaded Passage. Urshanabi, with a voice laden with gravity, instructs Gilgamesh on how to navigate through this perilous space, emphasizing a gentle and controlled progression to avoid disturbing the deadly waters.

With intense concentration, Gilgamesh follows Urshanabi's instructions to the letter. Each pole plunged into the briny abyss is a step further into the unknown, a struggle against the rising tension. Despite the oppressive silence and lack of landmarks, they advance, enveloped in the fog, as if they were the only living beings in a suspended world.

When Gilgamesh grabs the hundred and twentieth and final pole, a moment of doubt grips him. Thoughts swirl in his mind, suspecting Urshanabi of betrayal, considering a desperate act to defy the gods one last time. But in this critical moment, clarity returns. Gilgamesh realizes that his greatest battle is against himself, against the destructive impulse that haunts him.

With regained calm, he plunges the last pole into the water, maneuvering it with precision and quiet strength. And then, as if by magic, the fog disperses, revealing a clear sky and a welcoming shore. The ferry touches land in the long-sought country of Utnapishtim. This crossing, more than a physical journey, is an inner transformation for Gilgamesh, a passage from shadow to light, marking the beginning of a new chapter in his eternal quest.

On the desolate shore, Gilgamesh stands still, overwhelmed by disillusionment. Before him stretches a deserted beach, littered with ashes and petrified lava, leading to a parched land where only a few bushes and yellowed grasses dare to grow. The air is laden with a smell of rot, the landscape resembles a desert of abandonment.
"Such a place for the eternity of an immortal?" he exclaims with disdain. "This landscape is worthy of the deepest hells! The gods have played you for a fool, Utnapishtim!"

Eagerly disembarking, Gilgamesh steps onto the shore, his anger echoing the wind's whistles.
"Utnapishtim, enough with the secrecy! I implore you, show yourself immediately!"

"But I am right here," retorts a voice imbued with calm.
"Where? I do not see you."
"And yet, I see you very clearly."

Gilgamesh feels observed, almost manipulated, and his irritation intensifies.
"Your anger blinds you," the voice explains. "If only you could soothe it, even briefly... you would discover me."

This voice, both gentle and reassuring, gradually calms Gilgamesh's fury. As his anger subsides, the scene around him transforms: the beach lights up, the sand turns into fine gold, the oasis on the cliff blossoms before his eyes. Sheep graze peacefully under a light breeze that tempers the sun's ardor.
"Do you see? Nothing is simpler."

Utnapishtim then reveals himself, a man of modest stature, dressed in pure linen, his face evoking the clarity of a lively spring. His benevolent gaze welcomes Gilgamesh without judgment.
"What is your name, stranger? What do you seek here?"

Encouraged by Utnapishtim's attentive listening, Gilgamesh opens up without restraint, laying bare his tumultuous existence, marked by brutal authority, challenges issued, violence inflicted. He shares everything, not only his distress over the loss of his friend but also his own visceral fear of death.
"Here is my tale," he concludes. "I have exhausted my body in the trials of the mountain, my heart in the acceptance of my faults. I have donned the beast's skin, hoping to transform myself. I have struggled against myself to reach you. Here I am, give me the secret of immortality. I have surely earned it. I beg you, relieve my pain!"

Gilgamesh, already exhausted from his quests, stands before Utnapishtim, the immortal, his hope of discovering the secret to eternal life flickering like a flame in the wind. Utnapishtim observes the warrior devastated by his delusions, gauging the weight of his trials, his unwavering courage, but also his deep disarray in the face of the inevitable reality of the human condition. With gentle compassion and sincerity from the heart, he offers a hard truth to accept:
"Gilgamesh, there is nothing I can give you that you do not already possess."

These words, spoken with grave kindness, resonate in Gilgamesh like a clap of thunder, shaking the very foundations of his quest. Utnapishtim continues, his voice tinged with a bittersweet melancholy:
"Your destiny was written well before the dawn of your first day.

The power to change it is not mine. However, I invite you to contemplate more closely the story of your own existence."

Before Utnapishtim could finish speaking, Gilgamesh, consumed by desperate fury, lunges at him, demanding with the brute force that has always characterized him:
"Reveal this secret to me! Give it to me, or I will force you to divulge it!"

Suddenly, a storm breaks out, lightning streaks across the sky, and the air fills with the stench of decay. The earth begins to swarm with snakes while the peaceful sheep of the oasis transform into malevolent creatures. Gilgamesh, realizing the impossibility of his demand, releases Utnapishtim and prepares to fight the demons stirring around him.

It is then that Utnapishtim's voice rises above the tumult, a call to reason:
"This is not the way, Gilgamesh. You are delving further into error."

"Think, Gilgamesh! Look around you and reflect!" urges Utnapishtim, like a father guiding his son through trials.

At these words, Gilgamesh lowers his weapon, and calm returns. He then understands that the source of his suffering and rage is none other than himself.
"The chaos, the corruption, the violence... it's my heart."
Gilgamesh reflects on the lush garden of precious stones, a symbol of the best within him. Utnapishtim encourages him to choose the better path, to use his strength not for destruction but for building, to bring the best of himself to the world.

Utnapishtim's voice becomes firmer, highlighting Gilgamesh's misuse of his strength, a gift that has become his greatest obstacle. He shows him a neglected garden, a symbol of his own life forsaken for vain conquests and excessive ambitions.

"Isn't this the domain of a king?" asks Utnapishtim. "The gods entrusted you with a kingdom, not to leave it in neglect but to care for it, to reign with humanity."

Gilgamesh listens, moved by these words that awaken in him a buried knowledge. He then questions Utnapishtim about the possibility of accessing a different form of immortality, an immortality forged by righteous acts and the eternal memory left for future generations.

"But this immortality is not the same as yours!" Gilgamesh protests, faced with the inevitable truth of his own mortality.

Utnapishtim then reveals to him that his own immortality is the result of a past trial, the Flood, an ancient story that, if Gilgamesh wishes, could offer him another insight into life and death.

Thus, despite the disappointment and pains, Gilgamesh is offered a new perspective, a path toward wisdom and a deep understanding of his own being. Utnapishtim's tale of the Flood awaits Gilgamesh, promising to reveal hidden truths about existence, death, and perhaps, the way to achieve a form of immortality unique to the human condition.

16 The Tale of Survival and Transformation

In the modest dwelling of Utnapishtim, a haven of peace nestled on the riverbank, Gilgamesh and his host cross the threshold to discover a space surprising in its vastness, far more expansive than it appears from the outside. Utnapishtim's wife, with lunar grace, welcomes them with a warmth that illuminates the room with her generosity.

Utnapishtim, with disarming simplicity, introduces his companion, his partner in the incredible adventure of the Ark. Gilgamesh, intrigued by the mention of the Ark, is invited to sit down, to share a simple yet rejuvenating meal before the story of their survival through the Flood begins.

Utnapishtim then starts his tale. He was the king of Shuruppak, living a tranquil existence until one day, in the secrecy of his reed house, the voice of Ea, his god, reached him, entrusting him with a secret of grave importance: the announcement of a flood meant to annihilate humanity. The solution? Build an Ark, a refuge against the impending catastrophe.

The project seemed insane, but Utnapishtim's faith in his god was unshakable. He followed the divine instructions to the letter, demolishing his palace to reclaim the wood needed for the construction of the Ark, a gigantic structure designed to survive the end of the world. The details of the construction, the dimensions, the number of rooms, everything was dictated by Ea, each element laden with symbolism and promises.

The Ark was built with the help of a whole team of carpenters, each contributing to the erection of what would be their only hope of survival. The bitumen, for waterproofing, was chosen with care, its quantities revealing a profound cosmic significance linked to the sacred numbers of Heaven and Earth, thus marking the Ark as the cradle of a new humanity.

Thus, Utnapishtim confided in Gilgamesh, telling him how, guided by the wisdom and foresight of his god, he had accepted the heavy responsibility of preserving life through the ordeal of the Flood. A divine task, an act of absolute faith in the possibility of a renewal for man and earth.

The construction of the Ark was completed in record time, marking the beginning of an intense and moving preparation phase. Everyone, from the scribe to the gardener, the mason, and the fisherman, brought what was most dear to them, thus constituting a true ark of human knowledge and culture. This unique assembly, representative of the diversity and richness of human skills, was carefully embarked on the Ark, prepared to roll towards its riverine destiny.

A grand celebration took place, a joyful and melancholic echo of traditional festivities, but under the sign of an imminent farewell. When the signals announced the imminence of the Flood, Utnapishtim, with determination tinged with solemnity, undertook to gather a pair of every living species, assuring them a refuge in the immense structure he had erected. With his wife by his side, he sealed the entrance to their floating sanctuary, isolating themselves from the outside world in anticipation of the cataclysm.

The unleashing of the waters was of unprecedented violence, destroying everything in its path, leaving no chance for life as it was known. In this apocalyptic darkness, even the gods, surprised and frightened by the extent of the destruction they had unleashed, felt dread before the merciless entity that the Flood had become, asserting itself beyond any will but its own.

Aboard the Ark, Utnapishtim transformed into a guardian of peace and tranquility, traversing each level of the vessel to reassure and soothe the terrified animals, becoming a beacon of calm in the storm ravaging the world. Ascending along the central mast, he spread around him an aura of serenity, thus affirming his role as the new patriarch of a world in gestation, bearer of hope for a humanity to rebuild.

In the depths of Utnapishtim's modest hut, the atmosphere filled with a new energy, charged with stories and tales from the past. Utnapishtim, with a voice filled with wisdom and experience, unveiled the secrets of his survival, his transformation, and above all, his mission given by Ea, his protective god. The narrative captivated Gilgamesh, taking him far beyond his own quests, into a world where the actions of each resonated through time and space.

Each animal brought aboard the Ark was a promise, a seed of a future to be reinvented. With patience and dedication, Utnapishtim traversed the immense floating structure, soothing fears, teaching harmony, transforming chaos into a new order. The task was titanic, but carried by an unshakeable faith in life, and in the possibility of a new beginning.

When the Flood calmed and the waters receded, leaving behind them a world washed of its sins but emptied of its life, Utnapishtim and his wife were witnesses to a profound, almost sacred silence. The release of the birds was a powerful symbol, each carrying a message, a task, a hope. The raven, by its failure to return, signaled the beginning of a new era, a world ready to be repopulated, rebuilt on foundations of compassion, mutual aid, and respect.

But the joy of survival was quickly darkened by the wrath of Enlil, the god who had unleashed the cataclysm. The confrontation between the deities revealed the tensions and contradictions within the pantheon, but also a fundamental truth: humanity was essential to the world's balance, even in the eyes of those who had wished for its end.

Enlil's decision to make Utnapishtim and his wife immortal, while exiling them far from humanity, was a cruel paradox: eternal life, indeed, but at the cost of isolation, of absence of contact with their peers, with only their memories and hopes of a better world for company. This immortality was both a gift and a curse, a constant reminder that even in the blessings of the gods, lie trials and sacrifices.

Gilgamesh listened, absorbing every word, every emotion, gradually realizing that his quest for immortality might not be the ultimate goal, but rather a part of a much larger journey, a journey towards self-understanding, the value of life, and the importance of leaving a positive imprint on the world and future generations.

17 From Revelation to Redemption

In the intimacy of their humble home, Utnapishtim shared the wisdom of his incredible journey with Gilgamesh, a visitor thirsty for answers, for truth. Every word, every sigh from the storyteller seemed to imbue the atmosphere with a new density, plunging Gilgamesh into a tumultuous sea of thoughts. Despite the generosity of the welcome, a persistent tension remained, an unsatisfied quest raged within the warrior.

Gilgamesh, for his part, battled an internal storm, his thoughts crashing like waves against the walls of his mind. The vastness of his own journey seemed to shrink in the face of Utnapishtim's revelations, exacerbating an insatiable thirst for surpassing, a burning desire to transcend his mortal condition. Each word from Utnapishtim echoed as a mirror of his own tribulations but without offering the comfort of a resolution.

Utnapishtim, with infinite patience and unfathomable depth, then proposed a challenge, an experiment to probe Gilgamesh's soul, to test his capacity to embrace eternity. The immortal, in an almost paternal gesture of wisdom, invited the king on an inner journey, a quest for vigilance, a confrontation with the silence of his being.

Gilgamesh, with the fervor and impetuosity that characterized him, accepted the challenge with an assurance bordering on arrogance. The warrior, confident in his strength and will, embarked on this trial with an almost childlike lightness, unaware of the abysses it promised to explore.

The scene then transformed into a lesson in humility, a poignant reminder of human fragility. Gilgamesh, defeated by sleep, surrendered to the arms of Morpheus with disconcerting simplicity, betraying the immense gap between his aspirations and his deep nature.

Utnapishtim, observing the scene with a serenity tinged with melancholy, turned away, letting time and silence work. His wife, a lifelong companion, gently questioned the chosen path, the method, perhaps suggesting an immediate awakening, a direct confrontation with the reality of failure.

But the immortal, wise among the wise, insisted on the necessity of full and complete awareness for Gilgamesh. Only an awakening to the truth, even if painful, could offer the warrior the key to his own transformation, his evolution.

In this space suspended between the real and the imaginary, between the quest for immortality and the acceptance of the human condition, Gilgamesh was invited to contemplate the reflection of his own humanity, to recognize in sleep the ultimate symbol of his vulnerability, his finiteness.

Utnapishtim's decision to let the loaves accumulate, silent witnesses of Gilgamesh's failure, became a mirror of the inevitable reality: immortality, if it exists, is found not in the denial of our humanity but in the full and complete embrace of all that constitutes us, in the beauty of our ephemerality.

As Gilgamesh stood before Utnapishtim, the vastness of his quest seemed to condense into a moment of revelation. The words of the immortal, like drops of morning dew, gently infused into the troubled mind of the warrior, promising a wisdom that surpassed the trial of vigilance. The modest hut, in which they were, transformed into a sanctuary of ancient truths, where time seemed suspended.

The alignment of the loaves, marking the passage of days, became a calendar of failure, a silent testimony of Gilgamesh's inner struggle against his own nature. His reaction, a mix of surprise and dismay, outlined the contours of a painful but necessary realization. Death, this inseparable companion of life, crept into every fiber of his being, reminding him of the vanity of human efforts against the inevitable.

Utnapishtim's proposition, a simple but profound invitation to stay awake, took on irony in the context of their dialogue. Gilgamesh, with all the bravery and assurance of a king and warrior, accepts the challenge, not yet perceiving the symbolic scope of this task. His failure to remain vigilant, even in the sacred space of revelation, underscores the abyss between the desire for immortality and the reality of the human condition.

Gilgamesh's awakening, orchestrated by Utnapishtim, is a moment of raw truth. The loaves, witnesses to his involuntary sleep, erode the last bastion of his denial. The acceptance of his mortality is made in pain and resignation, a silent goodbye to the illusion of an endless life.

Utnapishtim's reaction, imbued with compassion yet firm, reaffirms the essential lesson of the story: immortality is not a quest for physical endurance or iron will but a harmony with the natural order of things. The wise man, by his discreet withdrawal, leaves Gilgamesh to the vastness of his own introspection, allowing him to contemplate the reality of his existence with newfound clarity.

Utnapishtim's wife, a figure of kindness and empathy, intervenes as a voice of conscience, reminding of the importance of hope and healing. Her suggestion about the Herb of Youth is not just a material gift to Gilgamesh but a symbol of the perpetual quest for renewal, of the inner struggle for a full and meaningful life.
Gilgamesh's departure, guided by Urshanabi, is a step towards redemption, towards reclaiming his lost humanity. The quest for the Herb of Youth, while appearing to be a new chase after an elusive goal, actually represents Gilgamesh's inner journey towards

a deep understanding of his own mortality, towards accepting life as an ephemeral but infinitely precious gift.

In this new phase of his journey, Gilgamesh no longer seeks to defeat death but to understand the value of every moment of life, to grasp the subtle fragrance of existence that reveals itself in the fragility of being. His quest for the Herb of Youth becomes a metaphor for the search for wisdom, a pilgrimage towards inner peace and the acceptance of finitude as the very condition that lends life its beauty and meaning.

On the shore, under an azure sky, Gilgamesh stood, scrutinizing the vastness before him, marked by rocks emerging like ancient guardians of the sea. With determination, he chose two, ripped them from the ground as if to defy the abyss itself, and placed them on his vessel. Then, propelled by an invisible breath, that of Utnapishtim, he crossed the terrifying Waters of Death to venture into the open waters, where the sea came back to life, oscillating between waves and winds.

Lost in the blue vastness, Gilgamesh pondered the direction to take. The echo of Utnapishtim's words came back to him: "Every quest begins with yourself." This was the mantra that had to guide his inner search. Closing his eyes, gathering himself amidst the chaos, finding inner peace seemed a Herculean task. Everything, from the lapping of the water to the wind caressing his hair, conspired to distract him, to pull him away from his center.

Yet, the memory of Enkidu, clear and powerful, showed him the way. Enkidu, his brother in arms and spirit, was the key. Enkidu, who had known how to become one with the elements, still taught him, beyond death, to harmonize with the universe. "Enkidu, guide my heart through this inner steppe," Gilgamesh pleaded, and his friend's spirit filled him, clarifying his thoughts, soothing his torments.

Under Enkidu's invisible guidance, Gilgamesh became one with the vessel, instinctively navigating towards his destiny. The intoxicating scent of jasmine, an undeniable sign of the presence of the Herb of Youth, permeated the air, guiding his senses to the ocean's depths. There, in that abyss, the treasure awaited.

With unshakable resolution, he dived into the depths, guided by an ethereal luminescence, until the Herb of Youth, shimmering with promises, offered itself to him. Despite the thorns that lacerated his skin, he seized it, ripping a piece of eternity with it, and surfaced, triumphant.

Back on the ferry, his trophy in hand, Gilgamesh proclaimed his victory over mortality. The Herb, laid at the prow of the ship, bathed in sunlight, symbolized a renewed life, a recovered hope. Urshanabi, a silent witness to this transcendent quest, now steered their return to solid ground, to Uruk, where Gilgamesh's destiny was to be fulfilled.

In this suspended moment, Gilgamesh contemplated the Herb of Youth, absorbing its essence, merging with it. It was no longer just a remedy against death but a sign of deep communion with life, with the universe. The pain of the thorns in his flesh was but a small price to pay for this sacred union, this promise of regained harmony.

And in this moment of revelation, Gilgamesh understood that the answer to his quest, the true secret of existence, had always resided within him, waiting for him to ask the right question. The discovery of the Herb of Youth was not the end of his search but the beginning of a deeper understanding of his own nature, his place in the cosmic order, his path to wisdom.

18 Gilgamesh's Final Journey

As they finally touched solid ground, Gilgamesh and Urshanabi faced a new odyssey, a jagged crossing of mountains and valleys that barred their way back. Throughout this ordeal, Gilgamesh's mind was bubbling with innovative ideas. He held the Herb of Youth in his hands, a treasure snatched from the marine abyss, and he was burning with the desire to share this gift with his people. "This is how I will make humanity triumph," he thought, embracing the words of Utnapishtim that resonated in his mind as a revelation.

"Upon my return," he confided to Urshanabi, "I will offer this miraculous herb to one of my subjects on the brink of death. This will be my gift to Uruk, a pledge of renewal. Then, I will entrust this plant to the care of my most learned gardeners. They will, I am certain, unlock the secrets of its propagation. Imagine, Urshanabi, gardens where the Herb of Youth blooms, within everyone's reach!"

His daydreams took on a grand scale, sketching a future where his people would enjoy eternal prosperity. When at last the silhouette of Uruk emerged on the horizon, framed by its majestic walls, Gilgamesh's heart raced with a bittersweet emotion. The prospect of returning to his city filled him with pride, but a wave of apprehension also gripped him. What if, during his absence, others had filled the void of his presence? The idea of reconnecting with the tumults of city life, with its intrigues and responsibilities, made him waver.

Then a temptation seized him: the desire to flee, to escape the burdens of the crown for absolute freedom. But this thought only brushed his mind. Deep down, he knew that Uruk awaited him, that his people counted on him.

"They still do not know the treasure I bring back to them," he murmured, eyeing the Herb of Youth affectionately. "Without me, they would never know this gift. I am about to transform their destiny."

The words of Utnapishtim came back to him, vibrating with new meaning: "You will be immortal, in the image of those who have magnified humanity..." Gilgamesh, heart filled with resolution, resumed his walk.

Near a pond, he was seized by the desire to purify himself, to don freshness before re-entering his city. He first washed the Herb of Youth, wishing to restore the luster lost during their journey. Then, carefully placing it on the bank, he immersed himself, promising a swift return to his precious companion.

Cradled by the waters, he surrendered to the tranquility of the moment, unaware of the drama unfolding. Suddenly, a serpent, a stealthy emissary of fate, emerged from the grass, stealing the Herb of Youth before disappearing as quickly as it had appeared. The discovery of this betrayal would mark Gilgamesh with an indelible scar, reminding him of the transience of all quests, the vanity of human hopes in the face of the relentless wheel of fate.

The shadowy figure of the serpent marked the end of a quest, leaving Gilgamesh devastated on the shore, facing the emptiness of his ephemeral triumph. In a flash, there he was, kneeling, his soul flayed by the theft of his hope. The reptile, in its subterranean retreat, had taken more than an herb; it had stolen a part of the future envisioned by Gilgamesh, leaving behind its worn skin as a cruel trophy of its victory.

Gilgamesh was a prisoner of his despair, his distress so profound that even the steppe seemed to hold its breath in echo to his pain. The night enveloped him, attempting in vain to veil his affliction, while an apparition, or perhaps a vision born of his tormented mind, offered him the presence of Utnapishtim. The face of the immortal, bearing an eternal tranquility, materialized before him, provoking a litany of bitter reproaches. Why reignite the spark of hope, only to cruelly snatch it away?

Utnapishtim's response, gentle and imbued with immutable wisdom, came not to soothe but to enlighten: the true quest was not for an unattainable eternity but for inner search, a journey into the depths of oneself. Gilgamesh, confronted with this revelation, traversed the night in introspection, meditating on the words of the immortal that merged with those of his past guides.

At dawn, the skin shed by the serpent, as a symbol of transformation, marked Gilgamesh's passage to a new existence. The loss of the Herb of Youth, far from being merely a defeat, proved to be a liberation, a lightening. The veil of fear and covetousness lifted, revealing to Gilgamesh the lightness of a renewed being, ready to welcome the innumerable possibilities of each moment.

His thoughts, now free from the grip of selfish desires, turned towards Uruk, his city, his people, his destiny as king. The vision of Uruk, emerging like a mirage, reminded him of his duty, his role. The bath in the pond, far from being a mere act of purification, symbolized his passage to rebirth, an acceptance of his mortality enriched by the wisdom gained.

The serpent, by stealing the Herb, had offered him the most precious lesson: true immortality does not lie in fleeing from death, but in the legacy one leaves, in the light one shares. Gilgamesh, finally at peace with himself, pronounced his assent to life, a resonant "yes" that sealed his commitment to his people and his own heart.

The voice of Utnapishtim, merged with those of Enkidu, Urshanabi,

Shamash, and even the Herb of Youth, carried the essence of all the lessons learned. "Every moment contains a spark": this truth, now anchored in his soul, guided Gilgamesh towards a future where every day would be a celebration of existence, a sharing of the inner light with his people. Uruk awaited him, not as a sovereign returning from exile, but as a new man, ready to infuse its veins with the breath of an eternity conquered not by flight, but by acceptance.

EPILOGUE

Gilgamesh walks towards the great gate of Uruk, his silhouette outlined against the horizon where the sun completes its journey, bathing the world in golden light. It is time for him to cross the threshold of his city, to return to the beating heart of his kingdom, to breathe into it the wisdom gained from a quest that was desperate and finally enlightening.

Twilight envelops the world, an invitation for us too to return to the haven of our own lives. Four millennia have passed since those distant days, but the echo of Gilgamesh still resonates, timeless, in the meanders of our collective memory. Immortal, he crosses the ages, accompanied by the faithful shadow of Enkidu, his alter ego, his soul brother. Together, they traverse eternity, watching over humanity with the tacit promise of indomitable strength, of love that defies death.

Their epic, woven from courage, pain, and redemption, continues to inspire us, a reminder of the unwavering power of friendship, sacrifice, and the relentless quest for meaning. Gilgamesh, in crossing the gates of Uruk, does not just return home; he enters into legend, offering to every soul that encounters his story a share of his immortality.

Thus, as the sun disappears behind the horizon, taking with it the last light of day, we retreat into the silence of our thoughts, accompanied by the indomitable spirit of Gilgamesh and the unwavering loyalty of Enkidu. Their voices, mingled with the twilight, whisper to us that, despite the centuries that separate us from their ancient world, their legacy remains, eternal and vibrant, at the heart of humanity.

Made in the USA
Las Vegas, NV
17 October 2024